FROM THE CRADLE TO THE GRAVE

'Fiction is like a spider's web, attached ever so slightly perhaps, but still attached to life at all four corners,' wrote Virginia Woolf, the famous English novelist.

This collection of short stories gives us portraits of people at intersections on the spider's web – fateful decisions of young people; victories, defeats, or revelations in the battlefield of marriage; the agonies of parents; the chance to start new relationships in middle age. The authors are all masters of the short-story genre, leading us effortlessly into imaginary worlds which feel as familiar as reality. Which of us does not recognize Angela, the youthful idealist in Waugh's story, or the scheming Mrs Bixby, or Maugham's smug Colonel?

The stories by Dahl and Maugham give us contrasting viewpoints on unsatisfactory marriages. Then we have two vivid portrayals of the effects of shock, through the very different styles of Sargeson and Carver. In the Bates and Hill stories we share the small miseries and cautious hopes of Miss Treadwell and Esme Fanshaw as they tremble on the brink of new relationships. Pictures of ordinary lives, caught for ever in the spider's web.

We begin with the pleasant tinkle of teaspoons on delicate porcelain teacups, under the sharp, sardonic eye of Saki . . .

ACKNOWLEDGEMENTS

The editors and publishers are grateful for permission to use the following copyright material:

'Same Time, Same Place' from *The Wild Cherry Tree* by H.E. BATES, published by Michael Joseph Ltd. Reprinted by kind permission of the Estate of H.E. Bates.

'The Bath' from *What We Talk About When We Talk About Love* by RAYMOND CARVER. Reprinted by permission of HarperCollins Publishers Ltd.

'Mrs Bixby and the Colonel's Coat' from *Kiss Kiss* by ROALD DAHL, published by Michael Joseph Ltd and Penguin Books Ltd. Reprinted by permission of Murray Pollinger.

'A Bit of Singing and Dancing' by SUSAN HILL from her collection entitled *A Bit of Singing and Dancing*. Reprinted by permission of Richard Scott Simon Ltd.

'The Colonel's Lady' from *Collected Short Stories Volume 2* by W. SOMERSET MAUGHAM. Copyright © by the Royal Literary Fund. Reprinted by permission of William Heinemann Ltd.

'They Gave her a Rise' by FRANK SARGESON from *The Stories of Frank Sargeson*. Reprinted by permission of Penguin Books (NZ) Ltd and the Frank Sargeson Memorial Trust.

'Mr Loveday's Little Outing' from *Work Suspended and other stories* by EVELYN WAUGH. Reprinted with the permission of the Peters Fraser & Dunlop Group Ltd.

FROM THE CRADLE TO THE GRAVE

Short Stories

EDITED BY
Clare West

SERIES ADVISERS
H.G. Widdowson
Jennifer Bassett

OXFORD UNIVERSITY PRESS

Oxford University Press
Walton Street, Oxford OX2 6DP

Oxford New York Toronto Madrid
Delhi Bombay Calcutta Madras Karachi
Kuala Lumpur Singapore Hong Kong Tokyo
Nairobi Dar es Salaam Cape Town
Melbourne Auckland
and associated companies in
Berlin Ibadan

OXFORD and OXFORD ENGLISH
are trade marks of Oxford University Press

ISBN 0 19 422692 1

This edition © Oxford University Press 1993

First published 1993
Third impression 1994

Typeset by Wyvern Typesetting Limited
Printed in England by Clays Ltd, St Ives plc

OXFORD BOOKWORMS
～ COLLECTION ～

FOREWORD

Texts of all kinds, including literary texts, are used as data for language teaching. They are designed or adapted and pressed into service to exemplify the language and provide practice in reading. These are commendable pedagogic purposes. They are not, however, what authors or readers of texts usually have in mind. The reason we read something is because we feel the writer has something of interest or significance to say and we only attend to the language to the extent that it helps us to understand what that might be. An important part of language learning is knowing how to adopt this normal reader role, how to use language to achieve meanings of significance to us, and so make texts our own.

The purpose of the *Oxford Bookworms Collection* is to encourage students of English to adopt this role. It offers samples of English language fiction, unabridged and unsimplified, which have been selected and presented to induce enjoyment, and to develop a sensitivity to the language through an appreciation of the literature. The intention is to stimulate students to find in fiction what Jane Austen found: 'the most thorough knowledge of human nature, the happiest delineation of its varieties, the liveliest effusions of wit and humour . . . conveyed to the world in the best chosen language.' (*Northanger Abbey*)

H.G. Widdowson
Series Adviser

OXFORD BOOKWORMS
∼ COLLECTION ∼

None of the texts has been abridged or simplified in any way, but each volume contains notes and questions to help students in their understanding and appreciation.

Before each story
- a short biographical note on the author
- an introduction to the theme and characters of the story

After each story
- *Notes* Some words and phrases in the texts are marked with an asterisk*, and explanations for these are given in the notes. The expressions selected are usually cultural references or archaic and dialect words unlikely to be found in dictionaries. Other difficult words are not explained. This is because to do so might be to focus attention too much on the analysis of particular meanings, and to disrupt the natural reading process. Students should be encouraged by their engagement with the story to infer general and relevant meaning from context.
- *Discussion* These are questions on the story's theme and characters, designed to stimulate class discussion or to encourage the individual reader to think about the story from different points of view.
- *Language Focus* These questions and tasks direct the reader's attention to particular features of language use or style.
- *Activities* These are suggestions for creative writing activities, to encourage readers to explore or develop the ideas and themes of the story in various imaginative ways.
- *Ideas for Comparison Activities* These are occasional additional sections with ideas for discussion or writing, which compare and contrast a number of stories in the volume.

CURRENT TITLES

From the Cradle to the Grave
Short stories by Saki, Evelyn Waugh, Somerset Maugham, Roald Dahl, Frank Sargeson, Raymond Carver, H.E. Bates, Susan Hill

Crime Never Pays
Short stories by Agatha Christie, Graham Greene, Ruth Rendell, Angela Noel, Dorothy L. Sayers, Margery Allingham, Arthur Conan Doyle, Patricia Highsmith

Contents

TEA

THE AUTHOR

Hector Hugh Munro, the British novelist and short-story writer known as Saki, was born in Burma in 1870 and brought up in England. He travelled widely and became a successful journalist; for six years he acted as correspondent for *The Morning Post* in Poland, Russia, and Paris. He is best known for his short stories, which are humorous, sometimes with a touch of black humour, and full of biting wit and bizarre situations. Some of his short-story collections are *Reginald in Russia and Other Sketches*, *The Chronicles of Clovis*, and *Beasts and Superbeasts*. He also published two novels, *The Unbearable Bassington* and *When William Came*. Saki was killed in France during the First World War, in 1916.

THE STORY

'It is a truth universally acknowledged that a single man in possession of a good fortune must be in want of a wife.' Thus wrote Jane Austen as the ironical first words of her famous novel *Pride and Prejudice*, and in the Edwardian England of Saki's day it was still thought that a man of good family had a duty to marry. To please himself, of course, but also to please his family and to satisfy the social conventions of the times.

James Cushat-Prinkly is a single man in possession of a good fortune, and his female relations and friends decide that he needs a wife. Cushat-Prinkly is a dutiful son, brother, nephew, and the idea of marriage is not disagreeable to him . . .

Tea

James Cushat-Prinkly was a young man who had always had a settled conviction that one of these days he would marry; up to the age of thirty-four he had done nothing to justify that conviction. He liked and admired a great many women collectively and dispassionately without singling out one for especial matrimonial consideration, just as one might admire the Alps without feeling that one wanted any particular peak as one's private property. His lack of initiative in this matter aroused a certain amount of impatience among the sentimentally minded women-folk of his home circle; his mother, his sisters, an aunt-in-residence, and two or three intimate matronly friends regarded his dilatory approach to the married state with a disapproval that was far from being inarticulate. His most innocent flirtations were watched with the straining eagerness which a group of unexercised terriers concentrates on the slightest movements of a human being who may be reasonably considered likely to take them for a walk. No decent-souled mortal can long resist the pleading of several pairs of walk-beseeching dog-eyes; James Cushat-Prinkly was not sufficiently obstinate or indifferent to home influences to disregard the obviously expressed wish of his family that he should become enamoured of some nice marriageable girl, and when his Uncle Jules departed this life and bequeathed him a comfortable little legacy it really seemed the correct thing to do to set about discovering someone to share it with him. The process of discovery was carried on more by the force of suggestion and the weight of public opinion than by any initiative of his own; a clear working majority of his female relatives and the aforesaid matronly friends had pitched on Joan Sebastable as the most suitable young woman in his range of acquaintance to whom he might propose marriage, and James became gradually accustomed to the idea that he and Joan would go together through the prescribed stages of congratulations, present-receiving, Norwegian or Mediterranean hotels, and eventual domesticity. It was necessary, however, to ask the lady what she thought about the matter; the family had so far conducted and directed the flirtation with ability and discretion, but the actual proposal would have to be an individual effort.

Cushat-Prinkly walked across the Park towards the Sebastable residence in a frame of mind that was moderately complacent. As the thing was going to be done he was glad to feel that he was going to get it settled and off his mind that afternoon. Proposing marriage, even to a nice girl like Joan, was a rather irksome business, but one could not have a honeymoon in Minorca and a subsequent life of married happiness without such preliminary. He wondered what Minorca was really like as a place to stop in; in his mind's eye it was an island in perpetual half-mourning, with black or white Minorca hens running all over it. Probably it would not be a bit like that when one came to examine it. People who had been in Russia had told him that they did not remember having seen any Muscovy ducks* there, so it was possible that there would be no Minorca fowls on the island.

His Mediterranean musings were interrupted by the sound of a clock striking the half-hour. Half-past four. A frown of dissatisfaction settled on his face. He would arrive at the Sebastable mansion just at the hour of afternoon tea. Joan would be seated at a low table, spread with an array of silver kettles and cream-jugs and delicate porcelain teacups, behind which her voice would tinkle pleasantly in a series of little friendly questions about weak or strong tea, how much, if any, sugar, milk, cream, and so forth. 'Is it one lump? I forgot. You do take milk, don't you? Would you like some more hot water, if it's too strong?'

Cushat-Prinkly had read of such things in scores of novels, and hundreds of actual experiences had told him that they were true to life. Thousands of women, at this solemn afternoon hour, were sitting behind dainty porcelain and silver fittings, with their voices tinkling pleasantly in a cascade of solicitous little questions. Cushat-Prinkly detested the whole system of afternoon tea. According to his theory of life a woman should lie on a divan or couch, talking with incomparable charm or looking unutterable thoughts, or merely silent as a thing to be looked on, and from behind a silken curtain a small Nubian page* should silently bring in a tray with cups and dainties*, to be accepted silently, as a matter of course, without drawn-out chatter about cream and sugar and hot water. If one's soul was really enslaved at one's mistress's* feet, how could one talk coherently about weakened tea! Cushat-Prinkly had never expounded his views on the subject to his mother; all her life she had been accustomed to tinkle pleasantly at tea-time behind dainty porcelain and silver, and if he had spoken to her about divans and Nubian pages she would have urged him to take a week's holiday at the seaside. Now, as he passed through a tangle of small streets that led indirectly to the elegant Mayfair* terrace for which he was bound, a horror at the idea of confronting Joan Sebastable at her tea-table seized on him. A momentary deliverance presented itself; on one floor of a narrow little house at the noisier end of Esquimault Street lived Rhoda Ellam, a sort of remote cousin, who made a living by creating hats out of costly materials. The hats really looked as if they had come from Paris; the cheques she got for them unfortunately never looked as if they were going to Paris. However, Rhoda appeared to find life amusing and to have a fairly good time in spite of her straitened circumstances. Cushat-Prinkly decided to climb up to her floor and defer by half-an-hour or so the important business which lay before him; by spinning out his visit he could contrive to reach the Sebastable mansion after the last vestiges of dainty porcelain had been cleared away.

Rhoda welcomed him into a room that seemed to do duty as workshop, sitting-room, and kitchen combined, and to be wonderfully clean and comfortable at the same time.

'I'm having a picnic meal,' she announced. 'There's caviar in that jar at your elbow. Begin on that brown bread-and-butter while I cut some more. Find yourself a cup; the teapot is behind you. Now tell me about hundreds of things.'

She made no other allusion to food, but talked amusingly and made her visitor talk amusingly too. At the same time she cut the bread-and-butter with a masterly skill and produced red pepper and sliced lemon, where so many women would merely have produced reasons and regrets for not having any. Cushat-Prinkly found that he was enjoying an excellent tea without having to answer as many questions about it as a Minister for Agriculture might be called on to reply to during an outbreak of cattle plague.

'And now tell me why you have come to see me,' said Rhoda suddenly. 'You arouse not merely my curiosity but my business instincts. I hope you've come about hats. I heard that you had come into a legacy the other day, and, of course, it struck me that it would be a beautiful and desirable thing for you to celebrate the event by buying brilliantly expensive hats for all your sisters. They may not have said anything about it, but I feel sure the same idea has occurred to them. Of course, with Goodwood* on us, I am rather rushed just now, but in my business we're accustomed to that; we live in a series of rushes – like the infant Moses*.'

'I didn't come about hats,' said her visitor. 'In fact, I don't think I really came about anything. I was passing and I just thought I'd look in and see you. Since I've been sitting talking to you, however, a rather important idea has occurred to me. If you'll forget Goodwood for a moment and listen to me, I'll tell you what it is.'

Some forty minutes later James Cushat-Prinkly returned to the bosom of his family, bearing an important piece of news.

'I'm engaged to be married,' he announced.

A rapturous outbreak of congratulation and self-applause broke out.

'Ah, we knew! We saw it coming! We foretold it weeks ago!'

'I'll bet you didn't,' said Cushat-Prinkly. 'If anyone had told me at lunch-time today that I was going to ask Rhoda Ellam to marry me and that she was going to accept me, I would have laughed at the idea.'

The romantic suddenness of the affair in some measure compensated James's women-folk for the ruthless negation of all their patient effort and skilled diplomacy. It was rather trying to have to deflect their enthusiasm at a moment's notice from Joan Sebastable to Rhoda Ellam; but, after all, it was James's wife who was in question, and his tastes had some claim to be considered.

On a September afternoon of the same year, after the honeymoon in Minorca had ended, Cushat-Prinkly came into the drawing-room of his new house in Granchester Square. Rhoda was seated at a low table, behind a service of dainty porcelain and gleaming silver. There was a pleasant tinkling note in her voice as she handed him a cup.

'You like it weaker than that, don't you? Shall I put some more hot water to it? No?'

NOTES

Muscovy duck (p12)
 a type of duck which comes from South America (not Moscow)
Nubian page (p13)
 a Sudanese or Egyptian boy servant, usually black
dainties (p13)
 small, delicate cakes
mistress (p13)
 a woman loved and courted by a man, but in modern use a woman who
 has a sexual relationship outside marriage
Mayfair (p13)
 a fashionable and expensive district of London
Goodwood (p14)
 a race-course in the south of England, popular with fashionable society
 of the time; any woman of that society going to Goodwood would have
 wanted to wear a new hat
the infant Moses (p14)
 a Biblical character who as a baby was put in a basket and hidden among
 the bulrushes on the banks of the Nile

DISCUSSION

1 What impression does the author give of James Cushat-Prinkly's
   character in the first paragraph? How important is his character in
   the development of the story?

2 Did you find the ending predictable? If so, did that lessen your
   appreciation of the story?

3 Of the three main characters, James Cushat-Prinkly, Joan Sebastable,
   and Rhoda Ellam, who do you think got the best bargain? Why?

4 What do you think of the title of the story – *Tea*? Is the story really
   about tea, or is tea being used as a symbol for something else? If so,
   what?

LANGUAGE FOCUS

1 Saki's humorous style often produces complicated, formal, even
   pompous expressions. Can you put the following into ordinary, direct
   English?

always had a settled conviction (p11)
his home circle (p11)
his dilatory approach to the married state (p11)
far from being inarticulate (p11)
become enamoured of (p11)
departed this life (p11)
bequeathed him a comfortable little legacy (p11)
a clear working majority of his female relatives (p12)
the actual proposal would have to be an individual effort (p12)
straitened circumstances (p13)
the bosom of his family (p15)

2 Do you find the following quotations amusing? Why (or why not)?
Explain the 'surface' meaning, that is, what the character (James or
his relations) is thinking. What other interpretations do you think the
author is inviting us to take? Do any words or phrases suggest to you
the idea of mockery?

- *Proposing marriage, even to a nice girl like Joan, was a rather
  irksome business.* (p12)
- *If one's soul was really enslaved at one's mistress's feet, how could
  one talk coherently about weakened tea!* (p13)
- *. . . if he had spoken to her about divans and Nubian pages she
  would have urged him to take a week's holiday at the seaside.*
  (p13)
- *. . . but, after all, it was James's wife who was in question, and
  his tastes had some claim to be considered.* (p15)

ACTIVITIES

1 Imagine you are one of the 'aforesaid matronly friends' and have just
heard the unexpected news of James's engagement to Rhoda Ellam.
Write a letter to your best friend to pass on the information.

2 The story is told mostly from James's point of view. Describe his visit
to Rhoda, but this time from her point of view. You might begin like
this:

*That afternoon Rhoda received an unexpected visitor. James
Cushat-Prinkly appeared at her front door at about tea-time. Though
pleased to see him, she wondered what the reason was for his visit . . .*

Mr Loveday's
Little Outing

The Author

Evelyn Waugh was born in London in 1903, and in the 1930s was acknowledged as England's leading satirical novelist. Readers loved the witty and sophisticated style of his early novels, for example, *Decline and Fall*, *Vile Bodies*, and *A Handful of Dust*, which satirized the social excesses of upper-class life in the 1920s and 1930s. His humour became blacker in his later novels, and after becoming a Roman Catholic he also dealt with religious themes, as in *Brideshead Revisited*. He died in 1966.

The Story

How do you define madness? The definition changes according to the century or the society. Some people think that there is more insanity in the 'normal' world than inside a mental hospital. We joke about madness; we call somebody 'mad' when often what we really mean is that we don't agree with them. But madness can also be a serious and frightening subject.

Lady Moping and her daughter Angela are not mad. Lord Moping, Angela's father, has shown signs of madness, and he is locked up in the local mental hospital. On a visit to him, Angela meets another inmate, Mr Loveday, a kind gentle old man who is helping to look after her father. Angela thinks she has discovered a great injustice, and she embarks on a well-meaning campaign . . .

Mr Loveday's Little Outing

1

'You will not find your father greatly changed,' remarked Lady Moping, as the car turned into the gates of the County Asylum*.

'Will he be wearing a uniform?' asked Angela.

'No, dear, of course not. He is receiving the very best attention.'

It was Angela's first visit and it was being made at her own suggestion.

Ten years had passed since the showery day in late summer when Lord Moping had been taken away; a day of confused but bitter memories for her; the day of Lady Moping's annual garden party, always bitter, confused that day by the caprice of the weather which, remaining clear and brilliant with promise until the arrival of the first guests, had suddenly blackened into a squall. There had been a scuttle for cover; the marquee had capsized; a frantic carrying of cushions and chairs, a table-cloth lofted to the boughs of the monkey-puzzler, fluttering in the rain; a bright period and the cautious emergence of guests on to the soggy lawns; another squall; another twenty minutes of sunshine. It had been an abominable afternoon, culminating at about six o'clock in her father's attempted suicide.

Lord Moping habitually threatened suicide on the occasion of the garden party; that year he had been found black in the face, hanging by his braces in the orangery; some neighbours, who were sheltering there from the rain, set him on his feet again, and before dinner a van had called for him. Since then Lady Moping had paid seasonal calls at the asylum and returned in time for tea, rather reticent of her experience.

Many of her neighbours were inclined to be critical of Lord Moping's accommodation. He was not, of course, an ordinary inmate. He lived in a separate wing of the asylum, specially devoted to the segregation of wealthier lunatics. They were given every consideration which their foibles permitted. They might choose their own clothes (many indulged in the liveliest fancies), smoke the most expensive brands of cigars, and, on the anniversaries of their certification*, entertain any other inmates for whom they had an attachment to private dinner parties.

The fact remained, however, that it was far from being the most expensive kind of institution; the uncompromising address, 'County Home for Mental Defectives', stamped across the notepaper, worked on the uniforms of their attendants, painted, even, upon a prominent hoarding at the main entrance, suggested the lowest associations. From time to time, with less or more tact, her friends attempted to bring to Lady Moping's notice particulars of seaside nursing homes, of 'qualified practitioners with large private grounds suitable for the charge of nervous or difficult cases', but she accepted them lightly; when her son came of age he might make any changes that he thought fit; meanwhile she felt no inclination to relax her economical regime; her husband had betrayed her basely on the one day in the year when she looked for loyal support, and was far better off than he deserved.

A few lonely figures in great-coats were shuffling and loping about the park.

'Those are the lower-class lunatics,' observed Lady Moping. 'There is a very nice little flower garden for people like your father. I sent them some cuttings last year.'

They drove past the blank, yellow brick façade to the doctor's private entrance and were received by him in the 'visitors' room', set aside for interviews of this kind. The window was protected on the inside by bars and wire netting; there was no fireplace; when Angela nervously attempted to move her chair further from the radiator, she found that it was screwed to the floor.

'Lord Moping is quite ready to see you,' said the doctor.

'How is he?'

'Oh, very well, very well indeed, I'm glad to say. He had rather a nasty cold some time ago, but apart from that his condition is excellent. He spends a lot of his time in writing.'

They heard a shuffling, skipping sound approaching along the flagged passage. Outside the door a high peevish voice, which Angela recognized as her father's, said: 'I haven't the time, I tell you. Let them come back later.'

A gentler tone, with a slight rural burr*, replied, 'Now come along. It is a purely formal audience. You need stay no longer than you like.'

Then the door was pushed open (it had no lock or fastening) and Lord Moping came into the room. He was attended by an elderly little man with full white hair and an expression of great kindness.

'That is Mr Loveday who acts as Lord Moping's attendant.'

'Secretary,' said Lord Moping. He moved with a jogging gait and shook hands with his wife.

'This is Angela. You remember Angela, don't you?'

'No, I can't say that I do. What does she want?'

'We just came to see you.'

'Well, you have come at an exceedingly inconvenient time. I am very busy. Have you typed out that letter to the Pope* yet, Loveday?'

'No, my lord. If you remember, you asked me to look up the figures about the Newfoundland fisheries first?'

'So I did. Well, it is fortunate, as I think the whole letter will have to be redrafted. A great deal of new information has come to light since luncheon. A great deal ... You see, my dear, I am fully occupied.' He turned his restless, quizzical eyes upon Angela. 'I suppose you have come about the Danube. Well, you must come again later. Tell them it will be all right, quite all right, but I have not had time to give my full attention to it. Tell them that.'

'Very well, Papa.'

'Anyway,' said Lord Moping rather petulantly, 'it is a matter of secondary importance. There is the Elbe and the Amazon and the Tigris to be dealt with first, eh, Loveday? ... *Danube* indeed. Nasty little river. I'd only call it a stream myself. Well, can't stop, nice of you to come. I would do more for you if I could, but you see how I'm fixed. Write to me about it. That's it. *Put it in black and white.*'

And with that he left the room.

'You see,' said the doctor, 'he is in excellent condition. He is putting on weight, eating and sleeping excellently. In fact, the whole tone of his system is above reproach.'

The door opened again and Loveday returned.

'Forgive my coming back, sir, but I was afraid that the young lady might be upset at his Lordship's not knowing her. You mustn't mind him, miss. Next time he'll be very pleased to see you. It's only today he's put out on account of being behindhand with his work. You see, sir, all this week I've been helping in the library and I haven't been able to get all his Lordship's reports typed out. And he's got muddled with his card index. That's all it is. He doesn't mean any harm.'

'What a nice man,' said Angela, when Loveday had gone back to his charge.

'Yes, I don't know what we should do without old Loveday. Everybody loves him, staff and patients alike.'

'I remember him well. It's a great comfort to know that you are able to get such good warders,' said Lady Moping; 'people who don't know, say such foolish things about asylums.'

'Oh, but Loveday isn't a warder,' said the doctor.

'You don't mean he's cuckoo, too?' said Angela.

The doctor corrected her.

'He is an *inmate*. It is rather an interesting case. He has been here for thirty-five years.'

'But I've never seen anyone saner,' said Angela.

'He certainly has that air,' said the doctor, 'and in the last twenty years we have treated him as such. He is the life and soul of the place. Of course he is not one of the private patients, but we allow him to mix freely with them. He plays billiards excellently, does conjuring tricks at the concert, mends their gramophones, valets them, helps them in their crossword puzzles and various – er – hobbies. We allow them to give him small tips for services rendered, and he must by now have amassed quite a little fortune. He has a way with even the most troublesome of them. An invaluable man about the place.'

'Yes, but why is he here?'

'Well, it is rather sad. When he was a very young man he killed somebody – a young woman quite unknown to him, whom he knocked off her bicycle and then throttled. He gave himself up immediately afterwards and has been here ever since.'

'But surely he is perfectly safe now. Why is he not let out?'

'Well, I suppose if it was to anyone's interest, he would be. He has no relatives except a step-sister who lives in Plymouth. She used to visit him at one time, but she hasn't been for years now. He's perfectly happy here and I can assure you *we* aren't going to take the first steps in turning him out. He's far too useful to us.'

'But it doesn't seem fair,' said Angela.

'Look at your father,' said the doctor. 'He'd be quite lost without Loveday to act as his secretary.'

'It doesn't seem fair.'

2

Angela left the asylum, oppressed by a sense of injustice. Her mother was unsympathetic.

'Think of being locked up in a looney bin all one's life.'

'He attempted to hang himself in the orangery,' replied Lady Moping, *'in front of the Chester-Martins.'*

'I don't mean Papa. I mean Mr Loveday.'

'I don't think I know him.'

'Yes, the looney they have put to look after Papa.'

'Your father's secretary. A very decent sort of man, I thought, and eminently suited to his work.'

Angela left the question for the time, but returned to it again at luncheon on the following day.

'Mums, what does one have to do to get people out of the bin?'

'The bin? Good gracious, child, I hope that you do not anticipate your father's return *here.*'

'No, no. Mr Loveday.'

'Angela, you seem to me to be totally bemused. I see it was a mistake to take you with me on our little visit yesterday.'

After luncheon Angela disappeared to the library and was soon immersed in the lunacy laws as represented in the encyclopedia.

She did not re-open the subject with her mother, but a fortnight later, when there was a question of taking some pheasants over to her father for his eleventh Certification Party she showed an unusual willingness to run over with them. Her mother was occupied with other interests and noticed nothing suspicious.

Angela drove her small car to the asylum, and, after delivering the game, asked for Mr Loveday. He was busy at the time making a crown for one of his companions who expected hourly to be anointed Emperor of Brazil, but he left his work and enjoyed several minutes' conversation with her. They spoke about her father's health and spirits. After a time Angela remarked, 'Don't you ever want to get away?'

Mr Loveday looked at her with his gentle, blue-grey eyes. 'I've got very well used to the life, miss. I'm fond of the poor people here, and I think that several of them are quite fond of me. At least, I think they would miss me if I were to go.'

'But don't you ever think of being free again?'

'Oh yes, miss, I think of it – almost all the time I think of it.'

'What would you do if you got out? There must be *something* you would sooner do than stay here.'

The old man fidgeted uneasily. 'Well, miss, it sounds ungrateful, but I can't deny I should welcome a little outing once, before I get too old to enjoy it. I expect we all have our secret ambitions, and there *is* one thing I often wish I could do. You mustn't ask me what ... It wouldn't take long. But I do feel that if I had done it just for a day, an afternoon even, then I would die quiet. I could settle down again easier, and devote myself to the poor crazed people here with a better heart. Yes, I do feel that.'

There were tears in Angela's eyes that afternoon as she drove away. 'He *shall* have his little outing, bless him,' she said.

3

From that day onwards for many weeks Angela had a new purpose in life. She moved about the ordinary routine of her home with an abstracted air and an unfamiliar, reserved courtesy which greatly disconcerted Lady Moping.

'I believe the child's in love. I only pray that it isn't that uncouth Egbertson boy.'

She read a great deal in the library, she cross-examined any guests who had pretensions to legal or medical knowledge, she showed extreme goodwill to old Sir Roderick Lane-Foscote, their Member*. The names 'alienist'*, 'barrister' or 'government official' now had for her the glamour that formerly surrounded film actors and professional wrestlers. She was a woman with a cause, and before the end of the hunting season she had triumphed. Mr Loveday achieved his liberty.

The doctor at the asylum showed reluctance but no real opposition. Sir Roderick wrote to the Home Office*. The necessary papers were signed, and at last the day came when Mr Loveday took leave of the home where he had spent such long and useful years.

His departure was marked by some ceremony. Angela and Sir Roderick Lane-Foscote sat with the doctors on the stage of the gymnasium. Below them was assembled everyone in the institution who was thought to be stable enough to endure the excitement.

Lord Moping, with a few suitable expressions of regret, presented Mr Loveday on behalf of the wealthier lunatics with a gold cigarette case; those who supposed themselves to be emperors showered him with decorations and titles of honour. The warders gave him a silver watch and many of the non-paying inmates were in tears on the day of the presentation.

The doctor made the main speech of the afternoon. 'Remember,' he remarked, 'that you leave behind you nothing but our warmest good wishes. You are bound to us by ties that none will forget. Time will only deepen our sense of debt to you. If at any time in the future you should grow tired of your life in the world, there will always be a welcome for you here. Your post will be open.'

A dozen or so variously afflicted lunatics hopped and skipped after him down the drive until the iron gates opened and Mr Loveday stepped into his freedom. His small trunk had already gone to the station; he elected to walk. He had been reticent about his plans, but he was well provided with money, and the general impression was that he would go to London and enjoy himself a little before visiting his step-sister in Plymouth.

It was to the surprise of all that he returned within two hours of his liberation. He was smiling whimsically, a gentle self-regarding smile of reminiscence.

'I have come back,' he informed the doctor. 'I think that now I shall be here for good.'

'But, Loveday, what a short holiday. I'm afraid that you have hardly enjoyed yourself at all.'

'Oh yes, sir, thank you, I've enjoyed myself *very much*. I'd been promising myself one little treat, all these years. It was short, sir, but *most* enjoyable. Now I shall be able to settle down again to my work here without any regrets.'

Half a mile up the road from the asylum gates, they later discovered an abandoned bicycle. It was a lady's machine of some antiquity. Quite near it in the ditch lay the strangled body of a young woman, who, riding home to her tea, had chanced to overtake Mr Loveday, as he strode along, musing on his opportunities.

NOTES

County Asylum (p20)
 The regional hospital for the care of mentally ill people; today, the word
 'hospital' is preferred to 'asylum'
certification (p21)
 the formal and official declaration of insanity
burr (p22)
 strong pronunciation of the 'r' sound, typical of certain English accents
the Pope (p22)
 the head of the Roman Catholic Church in Rome
Member (p27)
 a Member of Parliament; the elected representative in the government's
 House of Commons for that particular region
alienist (p27)
 a psychiatrist, especially a legal adviser on psychiatric problems
Home Office (p27)
 the British government department dealing with internal affairs

DISCUSSION

1 What does Lady Moping's treatment of her husband reveal about her
   own character? Do you feel more sympathy for her or for Lord
   Moping?

2 How mad do you think Lord Moping really is? Does the author intend
   us to think of another explanation for Lord Moping's behaviour?

3 What is your opinion of Angela's behaviour? Is she a naive idealist or
   an interfering busybody? Why does she ignore her father in favour of
   Mr Loveday? How do you think the author intends us to see Angela?

LANGUAGE FOCUS

1 There are a number of words in the story associated with madness or
   insanity. Make a list of them all and decide when it is appropriate or
   inappropriate to use each one.

2 What do the following remarks tell you about Lady Moping and her
   attitude to other people? What do they tell you about the author's
   attitude towards the upper classes?

- *Those are the lower-class lunatics. There is a very nice little flower garden for people like your father.* (p21)
- *He attempted to hang himself in the orangery*, in front of the Chester-Martins. (p25)
- *Your father's secretary. A very decent sort of man, I thought.* (p25)

ACTIVITIES

1 Imagine that you are one of the Chester-Martins at the garden party and witnessed Lord Moping's attempted suicide. Write a report of what you saw for the police.

2 Write Angela's letter to her Member of Parliament, explaining why Mr Loveday should be released.

3 How do you think Angela feels after Mr Loveday's little outing? Write her diary entry for the day after Mr Loveday returns to the asylum.

IDEAS FOR COMPARISON ACTIVITIES

1 These stories, *Tea* and *Mr Loveday's Little Outing*, both deal with young people who take an independent line, contrary to the expectations or advice of the older generation. Compare the reasons behind Angela's and James's decisions to take independent action.

2 Both stories end in either disillusionment or disaster. Do the authors wish to imply that young people should always take advice from their elders and betters? Or can you draw some other conclusion?

3 Both stories are written in humorous style. Did you find them funny? Is the overall tone light-hearted, or are the authors using humour to make serious comments or criticisms? Write a short paragraph on each story, summarizing what you think the authors' intentions are.

THE COLONEL'S LADY

THE AUTHOR

William Somerset Maugham was born in 1874. He originally qualified as a surgeon but soon became a full-time writer of plays, short stories, and novels. In both world wars he served as a British Intelligence agent, and travelled widely in the South Seas and the Far East, incorporating many of his experiences into his stories. He was a master storyteller and is still one of the most popular English authors of the twentieth century. Among his most famous novels are *Of Human Bondage*, *The Moon and Sixpence*, *Cakes and Ale*, and *The Razor's Edge*. He died in 1965.

THE STORY

The truth is generally thought to be a good thing; that is, when contrasted with a lie, which usually meets with moral disapproval. But the truth is sometimes uncomfortable, unwelcome, upsetting – especially in human relationships like marriage. And what is truth, anyway? Perhaps there are many kinds of truth, including what the English poet Keats called 'the truth of the imagination'.

Colonel George Peregrine does not usually trouble himself with questions like these. He is a decent, sensible fellow, a well-respected country landowner, leading a contented, conventional life. There is, however, one secret disappointment in his life – his wife Evie. She's a lady and a good wife, of course, but no longer attractive and, really, very dull . . .

THE COLONEL'S LADY

All this happened two or three years before the outbreak of the war.

The Peregrines were having breakfast. Though they were alone and the table was long they sat at opposite ends of it. From the walls George Peregrine's ancestors, painted by the fashionable painters of the day, looked down upon them. The butler brought in the morning post. There were several letters for the colonel, business letters, *The Times*, and a small parcel for his wife Evie. He looked at his letters and then, opening *The Times*, began to read it. They finished breakfast and rose from the table. He noticed that his wife hadn't opened the parcel.

'What's that?' he asked.

'Only some books.'

'Shall I open it for you?'

'If you like.'

He hated to cut string and so with some difficulty untied the knots.

'But they're all the same,' he said when he had unwrapped the parcel. 'What on earth d'you want six copies of the same book for?' He opened one of them. 'Poetry.' Then he looked at the title page. *When Pyramids Decay*, he read, by E.K. Hamilton. Eva Katherine Hamilton: that was his wife's maiden name. He looked at her with smiling surprise. 'Have you written a book, Evie? You are a slyboots.'

'I didn't think it would interest you very much. Would you like a copy?'

'Well, you know poetry isn't much in my line, but – yes, I'd like a copy, I'll read it. I'll take it along to my study. I've got a lot to do this morning.'

He gathered up *The Times*, his letters, and the book, and went out. His study was a large and comfortable room, with a big desk, leather armchairs, and what he called 'trophies of the chase' on the walls. On the bookshelves were works of reference, books on farming, gardening, fishing, and shooting, and books on the last war, in which he had won an MC and a DSO*. For before his marriage he had been in the Welsh Guards*. At the end of the war he retired and settled down to the life of a country gentleman in the spacious house, some twenty miles from Sheffield, which one of his forebears had built in the reign of George III. George Peregrine had an estate of some fifteen hundred acres which he managed with ability; he was a Justice of the Peace* and performed his duties conscientiously. During the season he rode to hounds two days a week. He was a good shot, a golfer, and though now a little over fifty he could still play a hard game of tennis. He could describe himself with propriety as an all-round sportsman.

He had been putting on weight lately, but was still a fine figure of a man; tall, with grey curly hair, only just beginning to grow thin on the crown, frank blue eyes, good features, and a high colour. He was a public-spirited man, chairman of any number of local organizations and, as became his class and station, a loyal member of the Conservative Party. He looked upon it as his duty to see to the welfare of the people on his estate and it was a satisfaction to him to know that Evie could be trusted to tend the sick and succour the poor. He had built a cottage hospital on the outskirts of the village and paid the wages of a nurse out of his own pocket. All he asked of the recipients of his bounty was that at elections, county or general, they should vote for his candidate. He was a friendly man, affable to his inferiors, considerate with his tenants, and popular with the neighbouring gentry. He would have been pleased and at the same time slightly embarrassed if someone had told him he was a jolly good fellow. That was what he wanted to be. He desired no higher praise.

It was hard luck that he had no children. He would have been an excellent father, kindly but strict, and would have brought up his sons as gentlemen's sons should be brought up, sent them to Eton*, you know, taught them to fish, shoot, and ride. As it was, his heir was a nephew, son of his brother killed in a motor accident, not a bad boy, but not a chip off the old block, no, sir, far from it; and would you believe it, his fool of a mother was sending him to a co-educational school. Evie had been a sad disappointment to him. Of course she was a lady, and she had a bit of money of her own; she managed the house uncommonly well and she was a good hostess. The village people adored her. She had been a pretty little thing when he married her, with a creamy skin, light brown hair, and a trim figure, healthy too, and not a bad tennis player; he couldn't understand why she'd had no children; of course she was faded now, she must be getting on for five and forty; her skin was drab, her hair had lost its sheen, and she was as thin as a rail. She was always neat and suitably dressed, but she didn't seem to bother how she looked, she wore no make-up and didn't even use lipstick; sometimes at night when she dolled herself up for a party, you could tell that once she'd been quite attractive, but ordinarily she was – well, the sort of woman you simply didn't notice. A nice woman, of course, a good wife, and it wasn't her fault if she was barren, but it was tough on a fellow who wanted an heir of his own loins; she hadn't any vitality, that's what was the matter with her. He supposed he'd been in love with her when he asked her to marry him, at least sufficiently in love for a man who wanted to marry and settle down, but with time he discovered that they had nothing much in common. She didn't care about hunting, and fishing bored her. Naturally they'd drifted apart. He had to do her the justice to

admit that she'd never bothered him. There'd been no scenes.
They had no quarrels. She seemed to take it for granted that he
should go his own way. When he went up to London now and
then she never wanted to come with him. He had a girl there,
well, she wasn't exactly a girl, she was thirty-five if she was a day,
but she was blonde and luscious and he only had to wire ahead
of time and they'd dine, do a show, and spend the night together.
Well, a man, a healthy normal man had to have some fun in his
life. The thought crossed his mind that if Evie hadn't been such a
good woman she'd have been a better wife; but it was not the sort
of thought that he welcomed and he put it away from him.

George Peregrine finished his *Times* and being a considerate
fellow rang the bell and told the butler to take it to Evie. Then he
looked at his watch. It was half past ten and at eleven he had
an appointment with one of his tenants. He had half an hour to
spare.

'I'd better have a look at Evie's book,' he said to himself.

He took it up with a smile. Evie had a lot of highbrow books
in her sitting-room, not the sort of books that interested him, but
if they amused her he had no objection to her reading them. He
noticed that the volume he now held in his hand contained no
more than ninety pages. That was all to the good. He shared
Edgar Allan Poe's* opinion that poems should be short. But as he
turned the pages he noticed that several of Evie's had long lines
of irregular length and didn't rhyme. He didn't like that. At his
first school, when he was a little boy, he remembered learning a
poem that began: *The boy stood on the burning deck*, and later,
at Eton, one that started: *Ruin seize thee, ruthless king*; and then
there was *Henry V**; they'd had to take that, one half. He stared
at Evie's pages with consternation.

'That's not what I call poetry,' he said.

Fortunately it wasn't all like that. Interspersed with the pieces that looked so odd, lines of three or four words and then a line of ten or fifteen, there were little poems, quite short, that rhymed, thank God, with the lines all the same length. Several of the pages were just headed with the word *Sonnet*, and out of curiosity he counted the lines; there were fourteen of them. He read them. They seemed all right, but he didn't quite know what they were all about. He repeated to himself: *Ruin seize thee, ruthless king.*

'Poor Evie,' he sighed.

At that moment the farmer he was expecting was ushered into the study, and putting the book down he made him welcome. They embarked on their business.

'I read your book, Evie,' he said as they sat down to lunch. 'Jolly good. Did it cost you a packet to have it printed?'

'No, I was lucky. I sent it to a publisher and he took it.'

'Not much money in poetry, my dear,' he said in his good-natured, hearty way.

'No, I don't suppose there is. What did Bannock want to see you about this morning?'

Bannock was the tenant who had interrupted his reading of Evie's poems.

'He's asked me to advance the money for a pedigree bull he wants to buy. He's a good man and I've half a mind to do it.'

George Peregrine saw that Evie didn't want to talk about her book and he was not sorry to change the subject. He was glad she had used her maiden name on the title page; he didn't suppose anyone would ever hear about the book, but he was proud of his own unusual name and he wouldn't have liked it if some damned penny-a-liner* had made fun of Evie's effort in one of the papers.

During the few weeks that followed he thought it tactful not to ask Evie any questions about her venture into verse, and she never referred to it. It might have been a discreditable incident that they had silently agreed not to mention. But then a strange thing

happened. He had to go to London on business and he took
Daphne out to dinner. That was the name of the girl with whom
he was in the habit of passing a few agreeable hours whenever he
went to town.

'Oh, George,' she said, 'is that your wife who's written a book
they're all talking about?'

'What on earth d'you mean?'

'Well, there's a fellow I know who's a critic. He took me out
to dinner the other night and he had a book with him. "Got
anything for me to read?" I said. "What's that?" "Oh, I don't
think that's your cup of tea," he said. "It's poetry. I've just been
reviewing it." "No poetry for me," I said. "It's about the hottest
stuff I ever read," he said. "Selling like hot cakes. And it's damned
good." '

'Who's the book by?' asked George.

'A woman called Hamilton. My friend told me that wasn't her
real name. He said her real name was Peregrine. "Funny," I said,
"I know a fellow called Peregrine." "Colonel in the army," he
said. "Lives near Sheffield." '

'I'd just as soon you didn't talk about me to your friends,' said
George with a frown of vexation.

'Keep your shirt on, dearie. Who d'you take me for? I just said:
"It's not the same one." ' Daphne giggled. 'My friend said: "They
say he's a regular Colonel Blimp*." '

George had a keen sense of humour.

'You could tell them better than that,' he laughed. 'If my wife
had written a book I'd be the first to know about it, wouldn't I?'

'I suppose you would.'

Anyhow the matter didn't interest her and when the colonel
began to talk of other things she forgot about it. He put it out of
his mind too. There was nothing to it, he decided, and that silly
fool of a critic had just been pulling Daphne's leg. He was amused

at the thought of her tackling that book because she had been told it was hot stuff and then finding it just a lot of bosh cut up into unequal lines.

He was a member of several clubs and next day he thought he'd lunch at one in St James's Street. He was catching a train back to Sheffield early in the afternoon. He was sitting in a comfortable armchair having a glass of sherry before going into the dining-room when an old friend came up to him.

'Well, old boy, how's life?' he said. 'How d'you like being the husband of a celebrity?'

George Peregrine looked at his friend. He thought he saw an amused twinkle in his eyes.

'I don't know what you're talking about,' he answered.

'Come off it, George. Everyone knows E.K. Hamilton is your wife. Not often a book of verse has a success like that. Look here, Henry Dashwood is lunching with me. He'd like to meet you.'

'Who the devil is Henry Dashwood and why should he want to meet me?'

'Oh, my dear fellow, what do you do with yourself all the time in the country? Henry's about the best critic we've got. He wrote a wonderful review of Evie's book. D'you mean to say she didn't show it you?'

Before George could answer his friend had called a man over. A tall, thin man, with a high forehead, a beard, a long nose, and a stoop, just the sort of man whom George was prepared to dislike at first sight. Introductions were effected. Henry Dashwood sat down.

'Is Mrs Peregrine in London by any chance? I should very much like to meet her,' he said.

'No, my wife doesn't like London. She prefers the country,' said George stiffly.

'She wrote me a very nice letter about my review. I was pleased.

You know, we critics get more kicks than halfpence. I was simply bowled over by her book. It's so fresh and original, very modern without being obscure. She seems to be as much at her ease in free verse as in the classical metres.' Then because he was a critic he thought he should criticize. 'Sometimes her ear is a trifle at fault, but you can say the same of Emily Dickinson*. There are several of those short lyrics of hers that might have been written by Landor*.'

All this was gibberish to George Peregrine. The man was nothing but a disgusting highbrow. But the colonel had good manners and he answered with proper civility: Henry Dashwood went on as though he hadn't spoken.

'But what makes the book so outstanding is the passion that throbs in every line. So many of these young poets are so anaemic, cold, bloodless, dully intellectual, but here you have real naked, earthy passion; of course deep, sincere emotion like that is tragic – ah, my dear Colonel, how right Heine* was when he said that the poet makes little songs out of his great sorrows. You know, now and then, as I read and re-read those heart-rending pages I thought of Sappho*.'

This was too much for George Peregrine and he got up.

'Well, it's jolly nice of you to say such nice things about my wife's little book. I'm sure she'll be delighted. But I must bolt, I've got to catch a train and I want to get a bite of lunch.'

'Damned fool,' he said irritably to himself as he walked upstairs to the dining-room.

He got home in time for dinner and after Evie had gone to bed he went into his study and looked for her book. He thought he'd just glance through it again to see for himself what they were making such a fuss about, but he couldn't find it. Evie must have taken it away.

'Silly,' he muttered.

He'd told her he thought it jolly good. What more could a fellow be expected to say? Well, it didn't matter. He lit his pipe and read the *Field* till he felt sleepy. But a week or so later it happened that he had to go into Sheffield for the day. He lunched there at his club. He had nearly finished when the Duke of Haverel came in. This was the great local magnate and of course the colonel knew him, but only to say how d'you do to; and he was surprised when the Duke stopped at his table.

'We're so sorry your wife couldn't come to us for the weekend,' he said, with a sort of shy cordiality. 'We're expecting rather a nice lot of people.'

George was taken aback. He guessed that the Haverels had asked him and Evie over for the weekend and Evie, without saying a word to him about it, had refused. He had the presence of mind to say he was sorry too.

'Better luck next time,' said the Duke pleasantly and moved on.

Colonel Peregrine was very angry and when he got home he said to his wife:

'Look here, what's this about our being asked over to Haverel? Why on earth did you say we couldn't go? We've never been asked before and it's the best shooting in the county.'

'I didn't think of that. I thought it would only bore you.'

'Damn it all, you might at least have asked me if I wanted to go.'

'I'm sorry.'

He looked at her closely. There was something in her expression that he didn't quite understand. He frowned.

'I suppose *I* was asked?' he barked.

Evie flushed a little.

'Well, in point of fact you weren't.'

'I call it damned rude of them to ask you without asking me.'

'I suppose they thought it wasn't your sort of party. The Duchess is rather fond of writers and people like that, you know.

She's having Henry Dashwood, the critic, and for some reason he wants to meet me.'

'It was damned nice of you to refuse, Evie.'

'It's the least I could do,' she smiled. She hesitated a moment. 'George, my publishers want to give a little dinner party one day towards the end of the month and of course they want you to come too.'

'Oh, I don't think that's quite my mark. I'll come up to London with you if you like. I'll find someone to dine with.'

Daphne.

'I expect it'll be very dull, but they're making rather a point of it. And the day after, the American publisher who's taken my book is giving a cocktail party at Claridge's. I'd like you to come to that if you wouldn't mind.'

'Sounds like a crashing bore, but if you really want me to come I'll come.'

'It would be sweet of you.'

George Peregrine was dazed by the cocktail party. There were a lot of people. Some of them didn't look so bad, a few of the women were decently turned out, but the men seemed to him pretty awful. He was introduced to everyone as Colonel Peregrine, E.K. Hamilton's husband, you know. The men didn't seem to have anything to say to him, but the women gushed.

'You *must* be proud of your wife. Isn't it *wonderful*? You know, I read it right through at a sitting, I simply couldn't put it down, and when I'd finished I started again at the beginning and read it right through a second time. I was simply *thrilled*.'

The English publisher said to him:

'We've not had a success like this with a book of verse for twenty years. I've never seen such reviews.'

The American publisher said to him:

'It's swell. It'll be a smash hit in America. You wait and see.'

The American publisher had sent Evie a great spray of orchids. Damned ridiculous, thought George. As they came in, people were taken up to Evie, and it was evident that they said flattering things to her, which she took with a pleasant smile and a word or two of thanks. She was a trifle flushed with the excitement, but seemed quite at her ease. Though he thought the whole thing a lot of stuff and nonsense George noted with approval that his wife was carrying it off in just the right way.

'Well, there's one thing,' he said to himself, 'you can see she's a lady and that's a damned sight more than you can say of anyone else here.'

He drank a good many cocktails. But there was one thing that bothered him. He had a notion that some of the people he was introduced to looked at him in rather a funny sort of way, he couldn't quite make out what it meant, and once when he strolled by two women who were sitting together on a sofa he had the impression that they were talking about him and after he passed he was almost certain they tittered. He was very glad when the party came to an end.

In the taxi on their way back to their hotel Evie said to him:

'You were wonderful, dear. You made quite a hit. The girls simply raved about you: they thought you so handsome.'

'Girls,' he said bitterly. 'Old hags.'

'Were you bored, dear?'

'Stiff.'

She pressed his hand in a gesture of sympathy.

'I hope you won't mind if we wait and go down by the afternoon train. I've got some things to do in the morning.'

'No, that's all right. Shopping?'

'I do want to buy one or two things, but I've got to go and be photographed. I hate the idea, but they think I ought to be. For America, you know.'

He said nothing. But he thought. He thought it would be a shock to the American public when they saw the portrait of the homely, desiccated little woman who was his wife. He'd always been under the impression that they liked glamour in America.

He went on thinking, and next morning when Evie had gone out he went to his club and up to the library. There he looked up recent numbers of *The Times Literary Supplement*, the *New Statesman*, and the *Spectator*. Presently he found reviews of Evie's book. He didn't read them very carefully, but enough to see that they were extremely favourable. Then he went to the bookseller's in Piccadilly where he occasionally bought books. He'd made up his mind that he had to read this damned thing of Evie's properly, but he didn't want to ask her what she'd done with the copy she'd given him. He'd buy one for himself. Before going in he looked in the window and the first thing he saw was a display of *When Pyramids Decay*. Damned silly title! He went in. A young man came forward and asked if he could help him.

'No, I'm just having a look round.' It embarrassed him to ask for Evie's book and he thought he'd find it for himself and then take it to the salesman. But he couldn't see it anywhere and at last, finding the young man near him, he said in a carefully casual tone: 'By the way, have you got a book called *When Pyramids Decay*?'

'The new edition came in this morning. I'll get a copy.'

In a moment the young man returned with it. He was a short, rather stout young man, with a shock of untidy carroty hair and spectacles. George Peregrine, tall, upstanding, very military, towered over him.

'Is this a new edition then?' he asked.

'Yes, sir. The fifth. It might be a novel the way it's selling.'

George Peregrine hesitated a moment.

'Why d'you suppose it's such a success? I've always been told no one reads poetry.'

'Well, it's good, you know. I've read it meself.' The young man, though obviously cultured, had a slight Cockney accent, and George quite instinctively adopted a patronizing attitude. 'It's the story they like. Sexy, you know, but tragic.'

George frowned a little. He was coming to the conclusion that the young man was rather impertinent. No one had told him anything about there being a story in the damned book and he had not gathered that from reading the reviews. The young man went on:

'Of course it's only a flash in the pan, if you know what I mean. The way I look at it, she was sort of inspired like by a personal experience, like Housman was with *The Shropshire Lad**. She'll never write anything else.'

'How much is the book?' said George coldly to stop his chatter. 'You needn't wrap it up, I'll just slip it into my pocket.'

The November morning was raw and he was wearing a greatcoat.

At the station he bought the evening papers and magazines and he and Evie settled themselves comfortably in opposite corners of a first-class carriage and read. At five o'clock they went along to the restaurant car to have tea and chatted a little. They arrived. They drove home in the car which was waiting for them. They bathed, dressed for dinner, and after dinner Evie, saying she was tired out, went to bed. She kissed him, as was her habit, on the forehead. Then he went into the hall, took Evie's book out of his greatcoat pocket and going into the study began to read it. He didn't read verse very easily and though he read with attention, every word of it, the impression he received was far from clear. Then he began at the beginning again and read it a second time. He read with increasing malaise, but he was not a stupid man and when he had finished he had a distinct understanding of what it was all about. Part of the book was in free verse, part in conventional metres, but the story it related was coherent and plain to the meanest intelligence. It was the story of a passionate love affair between an older woman, married, and a young man. George Peregrine made out the steps of it as easily as if he had been doing a sum in simple addition.

Written in the first person, it began with the tremulous surprise of the woman, past her youth, when it dawned upon her that the young man was in love with her. She hesitated to believe it. She thought she must be deceiving herself. And she was terrified when on a sudden she discovered that she was passionately in love with him. She told herself it was absurd, with the disparity of age between them nothing but unhappiness could come to her if she yielded to her emotion. She tried to prevent him from speaking but the day came when he told her that he loved her and forced her to tell him that she loved him too. He begged her to run away with him. She couldn't leave her husband, her home; and what life could they look forward to, she an ageing woman, he so young? How could she expect his love to last? She begged him to have mercy on her. But his love was impetuous. He wanted her, he wanted her with all his heart, and at last trembling, afraid, desirous, she yielded to him. Then there was a period of ecstatic happiness. The world, the dull, humdrum world of every day, blazed with glory. Love songs flowed from her pen. The woman worshipped the young, virile body of her lover. George flushed darkly when she praised his broad chest and slim flanks, the beauty of his legs and the flatness of his belly.

Hot stuff, Daphne's friend had said. It was that all right. Disgusting.

There were sad little pieces in which she lamented the emptiness of her life when as must happen he left her, but they ended with a cry that all she had to suffer would be worth it for the bliss that for a while had been hers. She wrote of the long, tremulous nights they passed together and the languor that lulled them to sleep in one another's arms. She wrote of the rapture of brief stolen moments when, braving all danger, their passion overwhelmed them and they surrendered to its call.

She thought it would be an affair of a few weeks, but miraculously it lasted. One of the poems referred to three years having gone by without lessening the love that filled their hearts. It looked as though he continued to press her to go away with him, far away, to a hill town in Italy, a Greek island, a walled city in Tunisia, so that they could be together always, for in another of the poems she besought him to let things be as they were. Their happiness was precarious. Perhaps it was owing to the difficulties they had to encounter and the rarity of their meetings that their love had retained for so long its first enchanting ardour. Then on a sudden the young man died. How, when or where George could not discover. There followed a long, heartbroken cry of bitter grief, grief she could not indulge in, grief that had to be hidden. She had to be cheerful, give dinner-parties and go out to dinner, behave as she had always behaved, though the light had gone out of her life and she was bowed down with anguish. The last poem of all was a set of four short stanzas in which the writer, sadly resigned to her loss, thanked the dark powers that rule man's destiny that she had been privileged at least for a while to enjoy the greatest happiness that we poor human beings can ever hope to know.

It was three o'clock in the morning when George Peregrine finally put the book down. It had seemed to him that he heard Evie's voice in every line, over and over again he came upon turns of phrase he had heard her use, there were details that were as familiar to him as to her: there was no doubt about it; it was her own story she had told, and it was as plain as anything could be that she had had a lover and her lover had died. It was not anger so much that he felt, nor horror or dismay, though he was dismayed and he was horrified, but amazement. It was as inconceivable that Evie should have had a love affair, and a wildly passionate one at that, as that the trout in a glass case over the chimney piece in his study, the finest he had ever caught, should suddenly wag its tail. He understood now the meaning of the amused look he had seen in the eyes of that man he had spoken to at the club, he understood why Daphne when she was talking about the book had seemed to be enjoying a private joke, and why those two women at the cocktail party had tittered when he strolled past them.

He broke out into a sweat. Then on a sudden he was seized with fury and he jumped up to go and awake Evie and ask her sternly for an explanation. But he stopped at the door. After all, what proof had he? A book. He remembered that he'd told Evie he thought it jolly good. True, he hadn't read it, but he'd pretended he had. He would look a perfect fool if he had to admit that.

'I must watch my step,' he muttered.

He made up his mind to wait for two or three days and think it all over. Then he'd decide what to do. He went to bed, but he couldn't sleep for a long time.

'Evie,' he kept on saying to himself. 'Evie, of all people.'

They met at breakfast next morning as usual. Evie was as she always was, quiet, demure, and self-possessed, a middle-aged woman who made no effort to look younger than she was, a woman who had nothing of what he still called It. He looked at her as he hadn't looked at her for years. She had her usual placid serenity. Her pale blue eyes were untroubled. There was no sign of guilt on her candid brow. She made the same little casual remarks she always made.

'It's nice to get back to the country again after those two hectic days in London. What are you going to do this morning?'

It was incomprehensible.

Three days later he went to see his solicitor. Henry Blane was an old friend of George's as well as his lawyer. He had a place not far from Peregrine's and for years they had shot over one another's preserves. For two days a week he was a country gentleman and for the other five a busy lawyer in Sheffield. He was a tall, robust fellow, with a boisterous manner and a jovial laugh, which suggested that he liked to be looked upon essentially as a sportsman and a good fellow and only incidentally as a lawyer. But he was shrewd and worldly-wise.

'Well, George, what's brought you here today?' he boomed as the colonel was shown into his office. 'Have a good time in London? I'm taking my missus up for a few days next week. How's Evie?'

'It's about Evie I've come to see you,' said Peregrine, giving him a suspicious look. 'Have you read her book?'

His sensitivity had been sharpened during those last days of troubled thought and he was conscious of a faint change in the lawyer's expression. It was as though he were suddenly on his guard.

'Yes, I've read it. Great success, isn't it? Fancy Evie breaking out into poetry. Wonders will never cease.'

George Peregrine was inclined to lose his temper.

'It's made me look a perfect damned fool.'

'Oh, what nonsense, George! There's no harm in Evie's writing a book. You ought to be jolly proud of her.'

'Don't talk such rot. It's her own story. You know it and everyone else knows it. I suppose I'm the only one who doesn't know who her lover was.'

'There is such a thing as imagination, old boy. There's no reason to suppose the whole thing isn't made up.'

'Look here, Henry, we've known one another all our lives. We've had all sorts of good times together. Be honest with me. Can you look me in the face and tell me you believe it's a made-up story?'

Harry Blane moved uneasily in his chair. He was disturbed by the distress in old George's voice.

'You've got no right to ask me a question like that. Ask Evie.'

'I daren't,' George answered after an anguished pause. 'I'm afraid she'd tell me the truth.'

There was an uncomfortable silence.

'Who was the chap?'

Harry Blane looked at him straight in the eye.

'I don't know, and if I did I wouldn't tell you.'

'You swine. Don't you see what a position I'm in? Do you think it's very pleasant to be made absolutely ridiculous?'

The lawyer lit a cigarette and for some moments silently puffed it.

'I don't see what I can do for you,' he said at last.

'You've got private detectives you employ, I suppose. I want you to put them on the job and let them find everything out.'

'It's not very pretty to put detectives on one's wife, old boy, and besides, taking for granted for a moment that Evie had an affair, it was a good many years ago and I don't suppose it would be possible to find out a thing. They seem to have covered their tracks pretty carefully.'

'I don't care. You put the detectives on. I want to know the truth.'

'I won't, George. If you're determined to do that you'd better consult someone else. And look here, even if you got evidence that Evie had been unfaithful to you what would you do with it? You'd look rather silly divorcing your wife because she'd committed adultery ten years ago.'

'At all events I could have it out with her.'

'You can do that now, but you know just as well as I do that if you do she'll leave you. D'you want her to do that?'

George gave him an unhappy look.

'I don't know. I always thought she'd been a damned good wife to me. She runs the house perfectly, we never have any servant trouble; she's done wonders with the garden and she's splendid with all the village people. But damn it, I have my self-respect to think of. How can I go on living with her when I know that she was grossly unfaithful to me?'

'Have you always been faithful to her?'

'More or less, you know. After all, we've been married for nearly twenty-four years and Evie was never much for bed.'

The solicitor slightly raised his eyebrows, but George was too intent on what he was saying to notice.

'I don't deny that I've had a bit of fun now and then. A man wants it. Women are different.'

'We only have men's word for that,' said Harry Blane, with a faint smile.

'Evie's absolutely the last woman I'd have suspected of kicking over the traces. I mean, she's a very fastidious, reticent woman. What on earth made her write the damned book?'

'I suppose it was a very poignant experience and perhaps it was a relief to her to get it off her chest like that.'

'Well, if she had to write it why the devil didn't she write it under an assumed name?'

'She used her maiden name. I suppose she thought that was enough, and it would have been if the book hadn't had this amazing boom.'

George Peregrine and the lawyer were sitting opposite one another with a desk between them. George, his elbow on the desk, his cheek on his hand, frowned at his thought.

'It's so rotten not to know what sort of a chap he was. One can't even tell if he was by way of being a gentleman. I mean, for all I know he may have been a farm-hand or a clerk in a lawyer's office.'

Harry Blane did not permit himself to smile and when he answered there was in his eyes a kindly, tolerant look.

'Knowing Evie so well I think the probabilities are that he was all right. Anyhow I'm sure he wasn't a clerk in my office.'

'It's been a shock to me,' the colonel sighed. 'I thought she was fond of me. She couldn't have written that book unless she hated me.'

'Oh, I don't believe that. I don't think she's capable of hatred.'

'You're not going to pretend that she loves me.'

'No.'

'Well, what does she feel for me?'

Harry Blane leaned back in his swivel chair and looked at George reflectively.

'Indifference, I should say.'

The colonel gave a little shudder and reddened.

'After all, you're not in love with her, are you?'

George Peregrine did not answer directly.

'It's been a great blow to me not to have any children, but I've never let her see that I think she's let me down. I've always been kind to her. Within reasonable limits I've tried to do my duty by her.'

The lawyer passed a large hand over his mouth to conceal the smile that trembled on his lips.

'It's been such an awful shock to me,' Peregrine went on. 'Damn it all, even ten years ago Evie was no chicken and God knows she wasn't much to look at. It's so ugly.' He sighed deeply. 'What would *you* do in my place?'

'Nothing.'

George Peregrine drew himself bolt upright in his chair and he looked at Harry with the stern set face that he must have worn when he inspected his regiment.

'I can't overlook a thing like this. I've been made a laughing-stock. I can never hold up my head again.'

'Nonsense,' said the lawyer sharply, and then in a pleasant, kindly manner, 'listen, old boy: the man's dead; it all happened a long while back. Forget it. Talk to people about Evie's book, rave about it, tell 'em how proud you are of her. Behave as though you had so much confidence in her, you *knew* she could never have been unfaithful to you. The world moves so quickly and people's memories are so short. They'll forget.'

'I shan't forget.'

'You're both middle-aged people. She probably does a great deal more for you than you think and you'd be awfully lonely without her. I don't think it matters if you don't forget. It'll be all to the good if you can get it into that thick head of yours that there's a lot more in Evie than you ever had the gumption to see.'

'Damn it all, you talk as if I was to blame.'

'No, I don't think you were to blame, but I'm not so sure that Evie was either. I don't suppose she wanted to fall in love with this boy. D'you remember those verses right at the end? The impression they gave me was that though she was shattered by his death, in a strange sort of way she welcomed it. All through she'd been aware of the fragility of the tie that bound them. He died in the full flush of his first love and had never known that love so seldom endures; he'd only known its bliss and beauty. In her own bitter grief she found solace in the thought that he'd been spared all sorrow.'

'All that's a bit above my head, old boy. I see more or less what you mean.'

George Peregrine stared unhappily at the inkstand on the desk.

He was silent and the lawyer looked at him with curious, yet sympathetic, eyes.

'Do you realize what courage she must have had never by a sign to show how dreadfully unhappy she was?' he said gently.

Colonel Peregrine sighed.

'I'm broken. I suppose you're right; it's no good crying over spilt milk and it would only make things worse if I made a fuss.'

'Well?'

George Peregrine gave a pitiful little smile.

'I'll take your advice. I'll do nothing. Let them think me a damned fool and to hell with them. The truth is, I don't know what I'd do without Evie. But I'll tell you what, there's one thing I shall never understand till my dying day: what in the name of heaven did the fellow ever see in her?'

Notes

an MC and a DSO (p34)
 Military Cross and Distinguished Service Order; medals won for bravery
 in war
the Welsh Guards (p34)
 a famous military regiment in the British army
Justice of the Peace (p34)
 a person who is not trained as a lawyer but who acts as a judge (unpaid)
 in a local law court, which deals with less serious crimes
Eton (p35)
 a famous public school (fee-paying) for boys from upper-class families
Edgar Allan Poe (p36)
 an American writer famous for his poetry and short stories
Henry V (p36)
 a play by Shakespeare, often studied by schoolchildren
penny-a-liner (p37)
 (*derogatory*) a journalist who is paid by the number of lines written
Colonel Blimp (p38)
 (*derogatory*) a person who is ridiculously pompous and conservative
 (especially an old army officer)
Emily Dickinson, Landor, Heine, Sappho (p40)
 all famous poets (American, English, German, ancient Greek)
A Shropshire Lad (p45)
 a volume of lyric poems written by the English poet A.E. Housman

Discussion

1 George Peregrine knows that he and his wife have 'drifted apart'. Who
   do you blame for that? He had had the thought that 'if Evie hadn't
   been such a good woman she'd have been a better wife.' What do you
   think he means by that? What does it reveal about his attitude to
   women?

2 'There is such a thing as imagination,' says Henry Blane. Are you sure
   Evie had a lover? If so, what do you think would have happened if
   he hadn't died? If not, why did she write the poems?

3 Do you think George and Evie's relationship will be different from

now on? If so, how? From the point of view of their relationship, does it in fact matter whether there was a real lover or not?

LANGUAGE FOCUS

1 Find all the vocabulary and expressions in the story that show

- George Peregrine as a typical, very conventional country gentleman
- Evie as a woman who is no longer young or attractive.

2 Rephrase these colloquial expressions in your own words:

Did it cost you a packet? (p37)
I've half a mind to do it (p37)
I don't think that's your cup of tea (p38)
Selling like hot cakes (p38)
Hot stuff (p39)
Come off it (p39)
I must bolt (p40)
I must watch my step (p48)
All that's a bit above my head (p53)
It's no good crying over spilt milk (p54)

ACTIVITIES

1 Imagine that George did not take Henry Blane's advice, but went straight home to find out the truth from Evie. Write a new ending for the story. Does Evie decide to leave George, or do they agree to forget the past and stay together?

2 Imagine that you are a journalist from a 'gossip' magazine, and are interviewing George. Try to find out if George does in fact believe his wife had a love affair. George, having decided to follow Henry Blane's advice, tries hard to pretend that he doesn't believe it. Write the dialogue between George and the journalist.

3 Write a review of Evie's book for a Sheffield newspaper, mentioning that she is a local author.

MRS BIXBY AND THE COLONEL'S COAT

THE AUTHOR

Roald Dahl's parents were Norwegian, but he was born in Wales in 1916. He joined an expedition to explore Newfoundland, then worked for an oil company. He served in the Royal Air Force during the Second World War, and then in Intelligence. He started writing short stories, at first on flying themes, in 1942. His collections of short stories, *Someone Like You*, *Kiss Kiss*, and *Tales of the Unexpected* have been translated into many languages and are bestsellers all over the world. His storytelling is bizarre, alarming, and disturbing, always with a nasty sting in the tail. His children's books are also very popular. He died in 1990.

THE STORY

The institution of marriage always arouses strong opinions. Some writers see it as the ideal state for true love, some as a prison, others as a state of war, a never-ending battle of wits between husband and wife. 'The one charm of marriage', wrote Oscar Wilde, 'is that it makes a life of deception absolutely necessary for both parties.'

According to the narrator, marriage in North America provides a marvellous opportunity for women to enjoy themselves, while their unfortunate husbands slave away to pay their bills. Does the poor husband ever find out that his wife is deceiving him? Mrs Bixby is confident that Mr Bixby has no idea at all what really happens on her regular trips to Baltimore . . .

MRS BIXBY AND
THE COLONEL'S COAT

America is the land of opportunities for women. Already they own about eighty-five per cent of the wealth of the nation. Soon they will have it all. Divorce has become a lucrative process, simple to arrange and easy to forget; and ambitious females can repeat it as often as they please and parlay their winnings to astronomical figures. The husband's death also brings satisfactory rewards and some ladies prefer to rely upon this method. They know that the waiting period will not be unduly protracted, for overwork and hypertension are bound to get the poor devil before long, and he will die at his desk with a bottle of benzedrines in one hand and a packet of tranquillizers in the other.

Succeeding generations of youthful American males are not deterred in the slightest by this terrifying pattern of divorce and death. The higher the divorce rate climbs, the more eager they become. Young men marry like mice, almost before they have reached the age of puberty, and a large proportion of them have at least two ex-wives on the payroll by the time they are thirty-six years old. To support these ladies in the manner to which they are accustomed, the men must work like slaves, which is of course precisely what they are. But now at last, as they approach their premature middle age, a sense of disillusionment and fear begins to creep slowly into their hearts, and in the evenings they take to huddling together in little groups, in clubs and bars, drinking their whiskies and swallowing their pills, and trying to comfort one another with stories.

The basic theme of these stories never varies. There are always three main characters – the husband, the wife, and the dirty dog.

The husband is a decent clean-living man, working hard at his job. The wife is cunning, deceitful, and lecherous, and she is invariably up to some sort of jiggery-pokery with the dirty dog. The husband is too good a man even to suspect her. Things look black for the husband. Will the poor man ever find out? Must he be a cuckold for the rest of his life? Yes, he must. But wait! Suddenly, by a brilliant manoeuvre, the husband completely turns the tables on his monstrous spouse. The woman is flabbergasted, stupefied, humiliated, defeated. The audience of men around the bar smiles quietly to itself and takes a little comfort from the fantasy.

There are many of these stories going around, these wonderful wishful-thinking dreamworld inventions of the unhappy male, but most of them are too fatuous to be worth repeating, and far too fruity to be put down on paper. There is one, however, that seems to be superior to the rest, particularly as it has the merit of being true. It is extremely popular with twice- or thrice-bitten males in search of solace, and if you are one of them, and if you haven't heard it before, you may enjoy the way it comes out. The story is called 'Mrs Bixby and the Colonel's Coat', and it goes something like this:

Mr and Mrs Bixby lived in a smallish apartment somewhere in New York City. Mr Bixby was a dentist who made an average income. Mrs Bixby was a big vigorous woman with a wet mouth. Once a month, always on Friday afternoons, Mrs Bixby would board the train at Pennsylvania Station and travel to Baltimore to visit her old aunt. She would spend the night with the aunt and return to New York on the following day in time to cook supper for her husband. Mr Bixby accepted this arrangement good-naturedly. He knew that Aunt Maude lived in Baltimore, and that his wife was very fond of the old lady, and certainly it would be unreasonable to deny either of them the pleasure of a monthly meeting.

'Just so long as you don't ever expect me to accompany you,' Mr Bixby had said in the beginning.

'Of course not, darling,' Mrs Bixby had answered. 'After all, she is not *your* aunt. She's mine.'

So far so good.

As it turned out, however, the aunt was little more than a convenient alibi for Mrs Bixby. The dirty dog, in the shape of a gentleman known as the Colonel, was lurking slyly in the background, and our heroine spent the greater part of her Baltimore time in this scoundrel's company. The Colonel was exceedingly wealthy. He lived in a charming house on the outskirts of the town. No wife or family encumbered him, only a few discreet and loyal servants, and in Mrs Bixby's absence he consoled himself by riding his horses and hunting the fox.

Year after year, this pleasant alliance between Mrs Bixby and the Colonel continued without a hitch. They met so seldom – twelve times a year is not much when you come to think of it – that there was little or no chance of their growing bored with one another. On the contrary, the long wait between meetings only made the heart grow fonder, and each separate occasion became an exciting reunion.

'Tally-ho*!' the Colonel would cry each time he met her at the station in the big car. 'My dear, I'd almost forgotten how ravishing you looked. Let's go to earth.'

Eight years went by.

It was just before Christmas, and Mrs Bixby was standing on the station in Baltimore waiting for the train to take her back to New York. This particular visit which had just ended had been more than usually agreeable, and she was in a cheerful mood. But then the Colonel's company always did that to her these days. The man had a way of making her feel that she was altogether a rather remarkable woman, a person of subtle and exotic talents, fascinating beyond measure; and what a very different thing that was from the dentist husband at home who never succeeded in making her feel that she was anything but a sort of eternal patient, someone who dwelt in the waiting-room, silent among the magazines, seldom if ever nowadays to be called in to suffer the finicky precise ministrations of those clean pink hands.

'The Colonel asked me to give you this,' a voice beside her said. She turned and saw Wilkins, the Colonel's groom, a small wizened dwarf with grey skin, and he was pushing a large flattish cardboard box into her arms.

'Good gracious me!' she cried, all of a flutter. 'My heavens, what an enormous box! What is it, Wilkins? Was there a message? Did he send me a message?'

'No message,' the groom said, and he walked away.

As soon as she was on the train, Mrs Bixby carried the box into the privacy of the Ladies' Room and locked the door. How exciting this was! A Christmas present from the Colonel. She started to undo the string. 'I'll bet it's a dress,' she said aloud. 'It might even be two dresses. Or it might be a whole lot of beautiful underclothes. I won't look. I'll just feel around and try to guess what it is. I'll try to guess the colour as well, and exactly what it looks like. Also how much it cost.'

She shut her eyes tight and slowly lifted off the lid. Then she put one hand down into the box. There was some tissue paper on top; she could feel it and hear it rustling. There was also an envelope or a card of some sort. She ignored this and began burrowing underneath the tissue paper, the fingers reaching out delicately, like tendrils.

'My God,' she cried suddenly. 'It can't be true!'

She opened her eyes wide and stared at the coat. Then she

pounced on it and lifted it out of the box. Thick layers of fur made a lovely noise against the tissue paper as they unfolded, and when she held it up and saw it hanging to its full length, it was so beautiful it took her breath away.

Never had she seen mink like this before. It *was* mink, wasn't it? Yes, of course it was. But what a glorious colour! The fur was almost pure black. At first she thought it *was* black; but when she held it closer to the window she saw that there was a touch of blue in it as well, a deep rich blue, like cobalt. Quickly she looked at the label. It said simply, WILD LABRADOR MINK. There was nothing else, no sign of where it had been bought or anything. But that, she told herself, was probably the Colonel's doing. The wily old fox was making darn sure he didn't leave any tracks. Good for him. But what in the world could it have cost? She hardly dared to think. Four, five, six thousand dollars? Possibly more.

She just couldn't take her eyes off it. Nor, for that matter, could she wait to try it on. Quickly she slipped off her own plain red coat. She was panting a little now, she couldn't help it, and her eyes were stretched very wide. But oh God, the feel of that fur! And those huge wide sleeves with their thick turned-up cuffs! Who was it had once told her that they always used female skins for the arms and the male skins for the rest of the coat? Someone had told her that. Joan Rutfield, probably; though how *Joan* would know anything about *mink* she couldn't imagine.

The great black coat seemed to slide on to her almost of its own accord, like a second skin. Oh boy! It was the queerest feeling! She glanced into the mirror. It was fantastic. Her whole personality had suddenly changed completely. She looked dazzling, radiant, rich, brilliant, voluptuous, all at the same time. And the sense of power that it gave her! In this coat she could walk into any place she wanted and people would come scurrying around her like rabbits. The whole thing was just too wonderful for words!

Mrs Bixby picked up the envelope that was still lying in the box. She opened it and pulled out the Colonel's letter:

I once heard you saying you were fond of mink so I got you this. I'm told it's a good one. Please accept it with my sincere good wishes as a parting gift. For my own personal reasons I shall not be able to see you any more. Goodbye and good luck.

Well!

Imagine that!

Right out of the blue, just when she was feeling so happy.

No more Colonel.

What a dreadful shock.

She would miss him enormously.

Slowly, Mrs Bixby began stroking the lovely soft black fur of the coat.

What you lose on the swings you get back on the roundabouts.

She smiled and folded the letter, meaning to tear it up and throw it out of the window, but in folding it she noticed that there was something written on the other side:

PS. Just tell them that nice generous aunt of yours gave it to you for Christmas.

Mrs Bixby's mouth, at that moment stretched wide in a silky smile, snapped back like a piece of elastic.

'The man must be mad!' she cried. 'Aunt Maude doesn't have that sort of money. She couldn't possibly give me this.'

But if Aunt Maude didn't give it to her, then who did?

Oh God! In the excitement of finding the coat and trying it on, she had completely overlooked this vital aspect.

In a couple of hours she would be in New York. Ten minutes after that she would be home, and the husband would be there to greet her; and even a man like Cyril, dwelling as he did in a dark phlegmy world of root canals, bicuspids, and caries*, would start asking a few questions if his wife suddenly waltzed in from a weekend wearing a six-thousand-dollar mink coat.

You know what I think, she told herself. I think that goddam Colonel has done this on purpose just to torture me. He knew perfectly well Aunt Maude didn't have enough money to buy this. He knew I wouldn't be able to keep it.

But the thought of parting with it now was more than Mrs Bixby could bear.

'I've *got* to have this coat!' she said aloud. 'I've got to have this coat! I've got to have this coat!'

Very well, my dear. You shall have the coat. But don't panic. Sit still and keep calm and start thinking. You're a clever girl, aren't you? You've fooled him before. The man never has been able to see much further than the end of his own probe, you know that. So just sit absolutely still and *think*. There's lots of time.

Two and a half hours later, Mrs Bixby stepped off the train at Pennsylvania Station and walked quickly to the exit. She was wearing her old red coat again now and carrying the cardboard box in her arms. She signalled for a taxi.

'Driver,' she said, 'would you know of a pawnbroker that's still open around here?'

The man behind the wheel raised his brows and looked back at her, amused.

'Plenty along Sixth Avenue,' he answered.

'Stop at the first one you see, then, will you please?' She got in and was driven away.

Soon the taxi pulled up outside a shop that had three brass balls hanging over the entrance.

'Wait for me, please,' Mrs Bixby said to the driver, and she got out of the taxi and entered the shop.

There was an enormous cat crouching on the counter eating fishheads out of a white saucer. The animal looked up at Mrs Bixby with bright yellow eyes, then looked away again and went on eating. Mrs Bixby stood by the counter, as far away from the cat as possible, waiting for someone to come, staring at the watches, the shoe buckles, the enamel brooches, the old binoculars, the broken spectacles, the false teeth. Why did they always pawn their teeth, she wondered.

'Yes?' the proprietor said, emerging from a dark place in the back of the shop.

'Oh, good evening,' Mrs Bixby said. She began to untie the string around the box. The man went up to the cat and started stroking it along the top of its back, and the cat went on eating the fishheads.

'Isn't it silly of me?' Mrs Bixby said. 'I've gone and lost my pocketbook, and this being Saturday, the banks are all closed until Monday and I've simply got to have some money for the weekend. This is quite a valuable coat, but I'm not asking much. I only want to borrow enough on it to tide me over till Monday. Then I'll come back and redeem it.'

The man waited, and said nothing. But when she pulled out the mink and allowed the beautiful thick fur to fall over the counter, his eyebrows went up and he drew his hand away from the cat and came over to look at it. He picked it up and held it out in front of him.

'If only I had a watch on me or a ring,' Mrs Bixby said, 'I'd give you that instead. But the fact is I don't have a thing with me other than this coat.' She spread out her fingers for him to see.

'It looks new,' the man said, fondling the soft fur.

'Oh yes, it is. But, as I said, I only want to borrow enough to tide me over till Monday. How about fifty dollars?'

'I'll loan you fifty dollars.'

'It's worth a hundred times more than that, but I know you'll take good care of it until I return.'

The man went over to a drawer and fetched a ticket and placed it on the counter. The ticket looked like one of those labels you tie on to the handle of your suitcase, the same shape and size exactly, and the same stiff brownish paper. But it was perforated across the middle so that you could tear it in two, and both halves were identical.

'Name?' he asked.

'Leave that out. And the address.'

She saw the man pause, and she saw the nib of the pen hovering over the dotted line, waiting.

'You don't *have* to put the name and address, do you?'

The man shrugged and shook his head and the pen-nib moved on down to the next line.

'It's just that I'd rather not,' Mrs Bixby said. 'It's purely personal.'

'You'd better not lose this ticket, then.'

'I won't lose it.'

'You realize that anyone who gets hold of it can come in and claim the article?'

'Yes, I know that.'

'Simply on the number.'

'Yes, I know.'

'What do you want me to put for a description.'

'No description, either, thank you. It's not necessary. Just put the amount I'm borrowing.'

The pen-nib hesitated again, hovering over the dotted line beside the word ARTICLE.

'I think you ought to put a description. A description is always a help if you want to sell the ticket. You never know, you might want to sell it sometime.'

'I don't want to sell it.'

'You might have to. Lots of people do.'

'Look,' Mrs Bixby said. 'I'm not broke, if that's what you mean. I simply lost my purse. Don't you understand?'

'You have it your own way then,' the man said. 'It's your coat.'

At this moment an unpleasant thought struck Mrs Bixby. 'Tell me something,' she said. 'If I don't have a description on my ticket, how can I be sure you'll give me back the coat and not something else when I return?'

'It goes in the books.'

'But all I've got is a number. So actually you could hand me any old thing you wanted, isn't that so?'

'Do you want a description or don't you?' the man asked.

'No,' she said. 'I trust you.'

The man wrote 'fifty dollars' opposite the word VALUE on both sections of the ticket, then he tore it in half along the perforations and slid the lower portion across the counter. He took a wallet from the inside pocket of his jacket and extracted five ten-dollar bills. 'The interest is three per cent a month,' he said.

'Yes, all right. And thank you. You'll take good care of it, won't you?'

The man nodded but said nothing.

'Shall I put it back in the box for you?'

'No,' the man said.

Mrs Bixby turned and went out of the shop on to the street where the taxi was waiting. Ten minutes later, she was home.

'Darling,' she said as she bent over and kissed her husband. 'Did you miss me?'

Cyril Bixby laid down the evening paper and glanced at the

watch on his wrist. 'It's twelve and a half minutes past six,' he said. 'You're a bit late, aren't you?'

'I know. It's those dreadful trains. Aunt Maude sent you her love as usual. I'm dying for a drink, aren't you?'

The husband folded his newspaper into a neat rectangle and placed it on the arm of his chair. Then he stood up and crossed over to the sideboard. His wife remained in the centre of the room pulling off her gloves, watching him carefully, wondering how long she ought to wait. He had his back to her now, bending forward to measure the gin, putting his face right up close to the measurer and peering into it as though it were a patient's mouth.

It was funny how small he always looked after the Colonel. The Colonel was huge and bristly, and when you were near to him he smelled faintly of horseradish. This one was small and neat and bony and he didn't really smell of anything at all, except peppermint drops, which he sucked to keep his breath nice for the patients.

'See what I've bought for measuring the vermouth,' he said, holding up a calibrated glass beaker. 'I can get it to the nearest milligram with this.'

'Darling, how clever.'

I really must try to make him change the way he dresses, she told herself. His suits are just too ridiculous for words. There had been a time when she thought they were wonderful, those Edwardian jackets with high lapels and six buttons down the front, but now they merely seemed absurd. So did the narrow stovepipe trousers. You had to have a special sort of face to wear things like that, and Cyril just didn't have it. His was a long bony countenance with a narrow nose and a slightly prognathous* jaw, and when you saw it coming up out of the top of one of those tightly fitting old-fashioned suits it looked

like a caricature of Sam Weller*. He probably thought it looked
like Beau Brummell*. It was a fact that in the office he
invariably greeted female patients with his white coat
unbuttoned so that they would catch a glimpse of the trappings
underneath; and in some obscure way this was obviously meant
to convey the impression that he was a bit of a dog. But Mrs
Bixby knew better. The plumage was a bluff. It meant nothing.
It reminded her of an ageing peacock strutting on the lawn
with only half its feathers left. Or one of those fatuous
self-fertilizing flowers – like the dandelion. A dandelion never
has to get fertilized for the setting of its seed, and all those
brilliant yellow petals are just a waste of time, a boast, a
masquerade. What's the word the biologists use? Subsexual. A
dandelion is subsexual. So, for that matter, are the summer
broods of water fleas. It sounds a bit like Lewis Carroll*, she
thought – water fleas and dandelions and dentists.

'Thank you, darling,' she said, taking the martini and seating
herself on the sofa with her handbag on her lap. 'And what did
you do last night?'

'I stayed in the office and cast a few inlays. I also got my
accounts up to date.'

'Now really, Cyril, I think it's high time you let other people
do your donkey work for you. You're much too important for
that sort of thing. Why don't you give the inlays to the mechanic?'

'I prefer to do them myself. I'm extremely proud of my
inlays.'

'I know you are, darling, and I think they're absolutely
wonderful. They're the best inlays in the whole world. But I don't
want you to burn yourself out. And why doesn't that Pulteney
woman do the accounts? That's part of her job, isn't it?'

'She does do them. But I have to price everything up first. She
doesn't know who's rich and who isn't.'

'This Martini is perfect,' Mrs Bixby said, setting down her glass on the side table. 'Quite perfect.' She opened her bag and took out a handkerchief as if to blow her nose. 'Oh look!' she cried, seeing the ticket. 'I forgot to show you this! I found it just now on the seat of my taxi. It's got a number on it, and I thought it might be a lottery ticket or something, so I kept it.'

She handed the small piece of stiff brown paper to her husband, who took it in his fingers and began examining it minutely from all angles, as though it were a suspect tooth.

'You know what this is?' he said slowly.

'No dear, I don't.'

'It's a pawn ticket.'

'A what?'

'A ticket from a pawnbroker. Here's the name and address of the shop – somewhere on Sixth Avenue.'

'Oh dear, I *am* disappointed. I was hoping it might be a ticket for the Irish Sweep*.'

'There's no reason to be disappointed,' Cyril Bixby said. 'As a matter of fact this could be rather amusing.'

'Why could it be amusing, darling?'

He began explaining to her exactly how a pawn ticket worked, with particular reference to the fact that anyone possessing the ticket was entitled to claim the article. She listened patiently until he had finished his lecture.

'You think it's worth claiming?' she asked.

'I think it's worth finding out what it is. You see this figure of fifty dollars that's written here? You know what that means?'

'No, dear, what does it mean?'

'It means that the item in question is almost certain to be something quite valuable.'

'You mean it'll be worth fifty dollars?'

'More like five hundred.'

'Five hundred!'

'Don't you understand?' he said. 'A pawnbroker never gives you more than about a tenth of the real value.'

'Good gracious! I never knew that.'

'There's a lot of things you don't know, my dear. Now you listen to me. Seeing that there's no name and address of the owner . . .'

'But surely there's something to say who it belongs to?'

'Not a thing. People often do that. They don't want anyone to know they've been to a pawnbroker. They're ashamed of it.'

'Then you think we can keep it?'

'Of course we can keep it. This is now *our* ticket.'

'You mean *my* ticket,' Mrs Bixby said firmly. 'I found it.'

'My dear girl, what *does* it matter? The important thing is that we are now in a position to go and redeem it any time we like for only fifty dollars. How about that?'

'Oh, what fun!' she cried. 'I think it's terribly exciting, especially when we don't even know what it is. It could be *anything*, isn't that right, Cyril? Absolutely anything!'

'It could indeed, although it's most likely to be either a ring or a watch.'

'But wouldn't it be marvellous if it was a *real* treasure? I mean something *really* old, like a wonderful old vase or a Roman statue.'

'There's no knowing what it might be, my dear. We shall just have to wait and see.'

'I think it's absolutely fascinating! Give me the ticket and I'll rush over first thing Monday morning and find out!'

'I think I'd better do that.'

'Oh no!' she cried. 'Let *me* do it!'

'I think not. I'll pick it up on my way to work.'

'But it's *my* ticket! *Please* let me do it, Cyril! Why should *you* have all the fun?'

'You don't know these pawnbrokers, my dear. You're liable to get cheated.'

'I wouldn't get cheated, honestly I wouldn't. Give it to me, please.'

'Also you have to have fifty dollars,' he said, smiling. 'You have to pay out fifty dollars in cash before they'll give it to you.'

'I've got that,' she said. 'I think.'

'I'd rather you didn't handle it, if you don't mind.'

'But Cyril, *I found* it. It's mine. Whatever it is, it's mine, isn't that right?'

'Of course it's yours, my dear. There's no need to get so worked up about it.'

'I'm not. I'm just excited, that's all.'

'I suppose it hasn't occurred to you that this might be something entirely masculine – a pocket-watch, for example, or a set of shirt-studs. It isn't only women that go to pawnbrokers, you know.'

'In that case I'll give it to you for Christmas,' Mrs Bixby said magnanimously. 'I'll be delighted. But if it's a woman's thing, I want it myself. Is that agreed?'

'That sounds very fair. Why don't you come with me when I collect it?'

Mrs Bixby was about to say yes to this, but caught herself just in time. She had no wish to be greeted like an old customer by the pawnbroker in her husband's presence.

'No,' she said slowly. 'I don't think I will. You see, it'll be even more thrilling if I stay behind and wait. Oh, I do hope it isn't going to be something that neither of us wants.'

'You've got a point there,' he said. 'If I don't think it's worth fifty dollars I won't even take it.'

'But you said it would be worth five hundred.'

'I'm quite sure it will. Don't worry.'

'Oh, Cyril, I can hardly wait! Isn't it exciting?'

'It's amusing,' he said, slipping the ticket into his waistcoat pocket. 'There's no doubt about that.'

Monday morning came at last, and after breakfast Mrs Bixby followed her husband to the door and helped him on with his coat.

'Don't work too hard, darling,' she said.

'No, all right.'

'Home at six?'

'I hope so.'

'Are you going to have time to go to that pawnbroker?' she asked.

'My God, I forgot all about it. I'll take a cab and go there now. It's on my way.'

'You haven't lost the ticket, have you?'

'I hope not,' he said, feeling in his waistcoat pocket. 'No, here it is.'

'And you have enough money?'

'Just about.'

'Darling,' she said, standing close to him and straightening his tie, which was perfectly straight. 'If it happens to be something nice, something you think I might like, will you telephone me as soon as you get to the office?'

'If you want me to, yes.'

'You know, I'm sort of hoping it'll be something for you, Cyril. I'd much rather it was for you than for me.'

'That's very generous of you, my dear. Now I must run.'

About an hour later, when the telephone rang, Mrs Bixby was across the room so fast she had the receiver off the hook before the first ring had finished.

'I got it!' he said.

'You did! Oh, Cyril, what was it? Was it something good?'

'Good!' he cried. 'It's fantastic! You wait till you get your eyes on this! You'll swoon!'

'Darling, what is it? Tell me quick!'

'You're a lucky girl, that's what you are.'

'It's for me, then?'

'Of course it's for you. Though how in the world it ever got to be pawned for only fifty dollars I'll be damned if I know. Someone's crazy.'

'Cyril! Stop keeping me in suspense! I can't bear it!'

'You'll go mad when you see it.'

'What is it?'

'Try to guess.'

Mrs Bixby paused. Be careful, she told herself. Be very careful now.

'A necklace,' she said.

'Wrong.'

'A diamond ring.'

'You're not even warm. I'll give you a hint. It's something you can wear.'

'Something I can wear? You mean like a hat?'

'No, it's not a hat,' he said, laughing.

'For goodness sake, Cyril! Why don't you tell me?'

'Because I want it to be a surprise. I'll bring it home with me this evening.'

'You'll do nothing of the sort!' she cried. 'I'm coming right down there to get it now!'

'I'd rather you didn't do that.'

'Don't be so silly, darling. Why shouldn't I come?'

'Because I'm too busy. You'll disorganize my whole morning schedule. I'm half an hour behind already.'

'Then I'll come in the lunch hour. All right?'

'I'm not having a lunch hour. Oh well, come at one-thirty

then, while I'm having a sandwich. Goodbye.'

At half past one precisely, Mrs Bixby arrived at Mr Bixby's place of business and rang the bell. Her husband, in his white dentist's coat, opened the door himself.

'Oh, Cyril, I'm so excited!'

'So you should be. You're a lucky girl, did you know that?' He led her down the passage and into the surgery.

'Go and have your lunch, Miss Pulteney,' he said to the assistant, who was busy putting instruments into the sterilizer. 'You can finish that when you come back.' He waited until the girl had gone, then he walked over to a closet that he used for hanging up his clothes and stood in front of it, pointing with his finger. 'It's in there,' he said. 'Now – shut your eyes.'

Mrs Bixby did as she was told. Then she took a deep breath and held it, and in the silence that followed she could hear him opening the cupboard door and there was a soft swishing sound as he pulled out a garment from among the other things hanging there.

'All right! You can look!'

'I don't dare to,' she said, laughing.

'Go on. Take a peek.'

Coyly, beginning to giggle, she raised one eyelid a fraction of an inch, just enough to give her a dark blurry view of the man standing there in his white overalls holding something up in the air.

'Mink!' he cried. 'Real mink!'

At the sound of the magic word she opened her eyes quick, and at the same time she actually started forward in order to clasp the coat in her arms.

But there was no coat. There was only a ridiculous little fur neckpiece dangling from her husband's hand.

'Feast your eyes on that!' he said, waving it in front of her face.

Mrs Bixby put a hand up to her mouth and started backing

away. I'm going to scream, she told herself. I just know it. I'm going to scream.

'What's the matter, my dear? Don't you like it?' He stopped waving the fur and stood staring at her, waiting for her to say something.

'Why yes,' she stammered. 'I . . . I . . . think it's . . . it's lovely . . . really lovely.'

'Quite took your breath away for a moment there, didn't it?'

'Yes, it did.'

'Magnificent quality,' he said. 'Fine colour, too. You know something, my dear? I reckon a piece like this would cost you two or three hundred dollars at least if you had to buy it in a shop.'

'I don't doubt it.'

There were two skins, two narrow mangy-looking skins with their heads still on them and glass beads in their eye sockets and little paws hanging down. One of them had the rear end of the other in its mouth, biting it.

'Here,' he said. 'Try it on.' He leaned forward and draped the thing around her neck, then stepped back to admire. 'It's perfect. It really suits you. It isn't everyone who has mink, my dear.'

'No, it isn't.'

'Better leave it behind when you go shopping or they'll all think we're millionaires and start charging us double.'

'I'll try to remember that, Cyril.'

'I'm afraid you mustn't expect anything else for Christmas. Fifty dollars was rather more than I was going to spend anyway.'

He turned away and went over to the basin and began washing his hands. 'Run along now, my dear, and buy yourself a nice lunch. I'd take you out myself but I've got old man Gorman in the waiting-room with a broken clasp on his denture.'

Mrs Bixby moved towards the door.

I'm going to kill that pawnbroker, she told herself. I'm going right back there to the shop this very minute and I'm going to throw this filthy neckpiece right in his face and if he refuses to give me back my coat I'm going to kill him.

'Did I tell you I was going to be late home tonight?' Cyril Bixby said, still washing his hands.

'No.'

'It'll probably be at least eight-thirty the way things look at the moment. It may even be nine.'

'Yes, all right. Goodbye.' Mrs Bixby went out, slamming the door behind her.

At that precise moment, Miss Pulteney, the secretary-assistant, came sailing past her down the corridor on her way to lunch.

'Isn't it a gorgeous day?' Miss Pulteney said as she went by, flashing a smile. There was a lilt in her walk, a little whiff of perfume attending her, and she looked like a queen, just exactly like a queen in the beautiful black mink coat that the Colonel had given to Mrs Bixby.

NOTES

Tally-ho! (p61)
a hunting cry when the fox is seen

root canals, bicuspids, caries (p65)
technical words relating to teeth and dentistry

prognathous (p69)
sticking out, projecting (only of jaws)

Sam Weller (p70)
a famous humorous character in the novel *The Pickwick Papers* by
Charles Dickens

Beau Brummell (p70)
a real person; the elegantly dressed leader of fashion in nineteenth-
century London

Lewis Carroll (p70)
the author of *Alice's Adventures in Wonderland*, a famous children's
book about a dream world

the Irish Sweep (p71)
a kind of gambling (sweepstake) on a horse race by randomly
purchasing tickets

DISCUSSION

1 Compare what we know of the two men in Mrs Bixby's life.

2 Do you think Mr Bixby knows about his wife's relationship with the
   Colonel? If so, when and how do you think he found out?

3 Mrs Bixby's plan for keeping the mink coat does not work. What
   would you have done in her position? Can you think of a better plan?

4 What do you think Mrs Bixby will do, now that she knows her husband
   is unfaithful to her?

LANGUAGE FOCUS

1 'The plumage was a bluff.' Re-read this passage, where Mrs Bixby is
   thinking about her husband. Can you follow her train of thought, and
   explain the connection in her mind between a peacock, a dandelion,
   water fleas, and Lewis Carroll?

2   There are several expressions connected with these animals in the story:
    mice, dog, fox, rabbits, donkey. Can you find them and explain what
    they mean? Are these animals associated with similar ideas in your
    own language? Can you think of other animal expressions in English,
    e.g. lion-hearted, spidery writing, to smell a rat?

ACTIVITIES

1   What do you think are the Colonel's 'personal reasons' for not seeing
    Mrs Bixby any more? Write his diary for their last day together.

2   Imagine that while Cyril Bixby is talking to his wife about the pawn
    ticket, some quite different thoughts are going through his head. Read
    the conversation again and write down what he might be thinking.
    You could begin like this:

    *'So, you found a pawn ticket on the taxi seat, did you? And you
    don't even know what it is? Come, come, my dear, do you really
    expect me to believe that? Let's play a little game ...'*

3   Write a letter from Miss Pulteney to her best friend, explaining how
    she was given the mink coat.

IDEAS FOR COMPARISON ACTIVITIES

1   How similar are the two colonels in the stories *The Colonel's Lady*
    and *Mrs Bixby and the Colonel's Coat*?

2   George Peregrine and Mrs Bixby are both regularly unfaithful. Why
    do you think they feel this is normal for them but not for their partner,
    and why do they both assume that their partner could not possibly
    be unfaithful?

3   Do you feel sympathy for George Peregrine and Mrs Bixby, or do you
    feel they deserve what happens to them in the end?

4   Do you think men sympathize with Mr Bixby (as Roald Dahl tells us),
    whereas women feel for Evie Peregrine? What does this show about
    our prejudices? And does this affect our enjoyment of the stories?

5   Which of these stories did you like best, and why?

THEY GAVE HER A RISE

THE AUTHOR

Frank Sargeson was born in New Zealand in 1903. Although he had several different jobs, he devoted most of his energies to writing short stories and novels. An acute observer of people and situations, he describes them in few words, but with great sensitivity. His stories are written in simple, informal style, usually in the first person. His novels include *I Saw in my Dream*, *Memoirs of a Peon*, *The Hangover*, *Joy of the Worm*, *Man of England Now*, and *Sunset Village*. He died in 1982.

THE STORY

News of a disaster is always horrifying, but it brings a particular terror if we are afraid that someone we know might be involved. Is it human nature to hope for the best, or to fear the worst? Is uncertainty harder to bear than knowledge? At moments of fear like these we often make extravagant promises, to ourselves, to God, to anyone at all . . .

When Mrs Bowman hears the explosion from the ammunition factory and then the news that people have been killed, she immediately goes into a state of shock. Her lodger tries to calm her down, but Mrs Bowman knows, she just knows . . .

THEY GAVE HER A RISE

When the explosion happened I couldn't go and see where it was. I'd been working on the wharves, and a case had dropped on my foot. It put me on crutches for a fortnight.

I was boarding with Mrs Bowman down by the waterfront at the time. She was quite a good sort though a bit keen on the main chance. But I didn't blame her because her husband had cleared out, and to make ends meet she took on cleaning jobs several days a week.

Explosions are like fires, you can't tell how far off they are. But it was some explosion. Mrs Bowman and I were in the kitchen and the crockery rattled, and the dust came down off the light shade. Sally Bowman was working out at the ammunition factory, and Mrs Bowman never said anything but you could see she thought that's where it might have happened. Of course people were talking out in the street and the news came pretty quick.

It was out at the ammunition factory. And they said some of the hands had been blown to smithereens.

Mrs Bowman broke down.

She's dead, she said, I know she's dead.

Well, we couldn't do anything. I went over next door on my crutches and asked the people if they'd find out about Sally and whistle me. Then I'd break the news to Mrs Bowman.

I went back and Mrs Bowman was worse than ever. She'd been getting dinner at the time and she sat there with her head down on the table among the potato peelings. Her hair'd come all unput too, and she looked awful. But she wasn't crying, and you sort of wished she had've been.

She's dead, she said, I know she's dead.

She's not dead, I said.

I know she's dead.

Bull's wool*, I said, she's not dead.

Oh God, she said, why did I make her go and work in that factory?

I'll guarantee she's been lucky.

She's all I've got. And now she's dead.

If you don't look out you'll start believing it, I said.

It was no good. She went on a treat. I asked her if she'd like me to get one of the neighbours in but she said no.

I don't want to see nobody no more, she said. Sally's all I was living for, and now she's dead. She was a good girl, she said, she was good to her mother.

Sure, I said. Of course she was good to her mother. So she always will be.

She won't. She's dead.

I couldn't do anything. The worst of it was I had a sort of sick feeling that Sally had been blown up. She was only seventeen and a nice kid too. And Mrs Bowman was as good as a widow. It was tough all right.

Then Mrs Bowman started to pray.

Lord God Jesus, she said, give me back my baby. You know she's all I've got. Do please Jesus Christ Almighty give me back my baby. Please Jesus just this once. Darling Jesus I know I done wrong. I shouldn't ought to have made my Sally go and work in that factory. It was because of the money. I had to make her go, you know I did. But oh sweet Jesus if you'll only give me back my baby just this once I won't never do another wrong thing in my life. Without a word of lie I won't, so help me God.

She went on like that. It sounded pretty awful to me, that sort of praying. Because I'm a Doolan* myself, and Mrs Bowman was always down on the churches. You wouldn't have thought she had a spark of religion in her at all. Still, it was tough. And I felt like nothing on earth.

The next thing was Sally was brought home in a car, one of those big limousines too. The joker driving had been going home from golf and he'd volunteered. He had to help Sally out of the car and up the steps because she was just a jelly. Her hat was on crooked and she couldn't stop crying. Of course the neighbours all came round but I told them to shove off and come back later on.

Well, Mrs Bowman had kidded herself into believing that Sally had been blown to smithereens. So when Sally walked in she went properly dippy and carried on about her having come back from the dead. So I slung off at her* a bit for being dippy and banged about cheerful-like getting them a cup of tea. Sally wasn't hurt at all, but some of the girls had been killed so naturally she was upset. Anyhow I slapped her on the back just to show her mother it wasn't a ghost that had walked in, then Mrs Bowman began crying and you could see she felt better. So both of them sat there and cried until the tea was ready.

I can't believe my eyes, Mrs Bowman said, I thought you was dead.

Well, I'm not dead, Sally said.

I thought you was.

I thought I was too. There's Peg Watson, she's dead.

What a shame, Mrs Bowman said.

And Marge Andrews, she's dead too.

Poor Mrs Andrews.

Mum it was awful. It was just like the noise of something being torn. Something big. A wind sort of tore at you too. And then there was a funny smell.

Anyhow you're not dead. You've been spared.

That wind knocked me over. I thought I was dead then.

You've been spared.

Yes I know. But what about Peg Watson and Marge Andrews?

Poor Mrs Andrews, Mrs Bowman said.

Then Mrs Bowman roused on to me* for putting too much sugar in her tea.

I thought I'd never taste tea again, Sally said, not when I was knocked over I didn't.

Have another cup? I said.

Mr Doran, Mrs Bowman said, how ever much tea did you put in the teapot?

I made it strong, I said. I thought you'd like it strong.

Anyone would think we was millionaires, Mrs Bowman said.

Sally said she wasn't ever going back to work in the ammunition factory again.

Why not? Mrs Bowman asked. You could see she was feeling a lot better and she spoke quite sharp.

Well I'm not. You never got knocked over by that wind.

I've had things to put up with in my life. Yes I have.

I know you have, mum. But you never got knocked over by a wind like that.

You can't avoid accidents.

I know you can't. But what about Peg and Marge?

Isn't it a shame? Poor Mrs Andrews. Marge was getting more money than you, wasn't she?

Anyhow I'm not going back. So there.

Oh, indeed, young lady, Mrs Bowman said. So that's the way you're going to talk. Not going back! Will you tell me where our money's coming from if you're not? Huh! You'd sooner see your mother scrubbing floors, wouldn't you?

Listen mum, Sally said. Listen . . .

Well, I left them to it. I went over next door to talk to the people, and you could hear Sally and her mother squabbling from there.

Of course Sally wasn't off for long. And they gave her a rise.

NOTES

Bull's wool (p84)
  (*New Zealand slang*) nonsense, rubbish
Doolan (p84)
  (*derogatory New Zealand slang*) an Irish family name, which is used to
  mean a Roman Catholic
slung off at her (p85)
  (*New Zealand slang*) mocked her, made fun of her
roused on to me (p86)
  (*New Zealand slang*) started scolding me

DISCUSSION

1 Do you agree that Mrs Bowman is 'a bit keen on the main chance'?
   Find examples of her interest in money.

2 If you were Sally, would you have gone back to work in the factory
   after the accident? Why, or why not?

3 Mrs Bowman uses emotional blackmail in trying to persuade Sally to
   go back to the factory. What other arguments do you think she could
   have used to persuade her?

4 What is your reaction to this story? Do you sympathize with Mrs
   Bowman? Do you think the author is suggesting any criticism or
   disapproval of her attitude?

LANGUAGE FOCUS

1 There are a number of examples of ungrammatical speech in this story.
   Rewrite the following in correct grammatical form.

   you sort of wished she had've been (p83)
   I don't want to see nobody no more (p84)
   I know I done wrong (p84)
   I shouldn't ought to have made ... (p84)
   I won't never do another wrong thing (p84)
   I thought you was dead (p85)
   Anyone would think we was millionaires (p86)

2   Can you explain what these idiomatic expressions mean?

  she was quite a good sort (p83)
  her hair'd come all unput (p83)
  a nice kid (p84)
  Mrs Bowman was as good as a widow (p84)
  it was tough (p84)
  I felt like nothing on earth (p85)

ACTIVITIES

1   You are a journalist. Write a report of the explosion for the local
  newspaper, using the information given in the story.

2   Imagine that Sally decides not to go back to her job. Write a new
  ending for the story, in which Sally comes home and tells her mother
  the news. Try to imitate the author's simple, informal style. You might
  begin like this:

  *I'm never going back to the factory, Mum. I went in and told
  them today.*
  You did what? Mrs Bowman said. I don't believe my ears.

3   Think of a new title for the story with your ending.

THE BATH

THE AUTHOR

Raymond Carver was born in 1938 in the USA, and taught at various North American universities. He contributed to many literary magazines and won several awards for his poems and short stories. His writing is crisp and direct, focusing on ordinary working people. Often his characters are in a state of uncertainty or indecision, between jobs, for example, or in the middle of a divorce. His short stories have been collected in *Will You Please Be Quiet, Please?*, *What We Talk About When We Talk About Love*, *Cathedral*, and *Fires: Essays, Stories, Poems*. He died in 1988.

THE STORY

Shock does strange things to the mind. Thoughts become dislocated, out of focus. Everyday life suddenly seems unreal, remote, as though seen at the end of a long tunnel. How can the rest of the world go on living – catching buses, going to work, sleeping, eating meals? Words take on new meanings, or no meaning at all.

Scotty will be eight years old in two days' time. A chocolate birthday cake has been ordered, a party planned for the afternoon. And then the accident, on the way to school on the morning of the birthday . . .

THE BATH

Saturday afternoon the mother drove to the bakery in the shopping center. After looking through a loose-leaf binder with photographs of cakes taped onto the pages, she ordered chocolate, the child's favorite. The cake she chose was decorated with a spaceship and a launching pad under a sprinkling of white stars. The name SCOTTY would be iced on in green as if it were the name of the spaceship.

The baker listened thoughtfully when the mother told him Scotty would be eight years old. He was an older man, this baker, and he wore a curious apron, a heavy thing with loops that went under his arms and around his back and then crossed in front again where they were tied in a very thick knot. He kept wiping his hands on the front of the apron as he listened to the woman, his wet eyes examining her lips as she studied the samples and talked.

He let her take her time. He was in no hurry.

The mother decided on the spaceship cake, and then she gave the baker her name and her telephone number. The cake would be ready Monday morning, in plenty of time for the party Monday afternoon. This was all the baker was willing to say. No pleasantries, just this small exchange, the barest information, nothing that was not necessary.

Monday morning, the boy was walking to school. He was in the company of another boy, the two boys passing a bag of potato chips back and forth between them. The birthday boy was trying to trick the other boy into telling what he was going to give in the way of a present.

At an intersection, without looking, the birthday boy stepped off the curb, and was promptly knocked down by a car. He fell on his side, his head in the gutter, his legs in the road moving as if he were climbing a wall.

The other boy stood holding the potato chips. He was wondering if he should finish the rest or continue on to school.

The birthday boy did not cry. But neither did he wish to talk anymore. He would not answer when the other boy asked what it felt like to be hit by a car. The birthday boy got up and turned back for home, at which time the other boy waved goodbye and headed off for school.

The birthday boy told his mother what had happened. They sat together on the sofa. She held his hands in her lap. This is what she was doing when the boy pulled his hands away and lay down on his back.

Of course, the birthday party never happened. The birthday boy was in the hospital instead. The mother sat by the bed. She was waiting for the boy to wake up. The father hurried over from his office. He sat next to the mother. So now the both of them waited for the boy to wake up. They waited for hours, and then the father went home to take a bath.

The man drove home from the hospital. He drove the streets faster than he should. It had been a good life till now. There had been work, fatherhood, family. The man had been lucky and happy. But fear made him want a bath.

He pulled into the driveway. He sat in the car trying to make his legs work. The child had been hit by a car and he was in the hospital, but he was going to be all right. The man got out of the car and went up to the door. The dog was barking and the telephone was ringing. It kept ringing while the man unlocked the door and felt the wall for the light switch.

He picked up the receiver. He said, 'I just got in the door!'

'There's a cake that wasn't picked up.'

This is what the voice on the other end said.

'What are you saying?' the father said.

'The cake,' the voice said. 'Sixteen dollars.'

The husband held the receiver against his ear, trying to understand. He said, 'I don't know anything about it.'

'Don't hand me that*,' the voice said.

The husband hung up the telephone. He went into the kitchen and poured himself some whiskey. He called the hospital.

The child's condition remained the same.

While the water ran into the tub, the man lathered his face and shaved. He was in the tub when he heard the telephone again. He got himself out and hurried through the house, saying, 'Stupid, stupid,' because he wouldn't be doing this if he'd stayed where he was in the hospital. He picked up the receiver and shouted, 'Hello!'

The voice said, 'It's ready.'

The father got back to the hospital after midnight. The wife was sitting in the chair by the bed. She looked up at the husband and then she looked back at the child. From an apparatus over the bed hung a bottle with a tube running from the bottle to the child.

'What's this?' the father said.

'Glucose,' the mother said.

The husband put his hand to the back of the woman's head.

'He's going to wake up,' the man said.

'I know,' the woman said.

In a little while the man said, 'Go home and let me take over.'

She shook her head. 'No,' she said.

'Really,' he said. 'Go home for a while. You don't have to worry. He's sleeping, is all.'

A nurse pushed open the door. She nodded to them as she went to the bed. She took the left arm out from under the covers and put her fingers on the wrist. She put the arm back under the covers and wrote on the clipboard attached to the bed.

'How is he?' the mother said.

'Stable,' the nurse said. Then she said, 'Doctor will be in again shortly.'

'I was saying maybe she'd want to go home and get a little rest,' the man said. 'After the doctor comes.'

'She could do that,' the nurse said.

The woman said, 'We'll see what the doctor says.' She brought her hand up to her eyes and leaned her head forward.

The nurse said, 'Of course.'

The father gazed at his son, the small chest inflating and deflating under the covers. He felt more fear now. He began shaking his head. He talked to himself like this. The child is fine. Instead of sleeping at home, he's doing it here. Sleep is the same wherever you do it.

The doctor came in. He shook hands with the man. The woman got up from the chair.

'Ann,' the doctor said and nodded. The doctor said, 'Let's just see how he's doing.' He moved to the bed and touched the boy's wrist. He peeled back an eyelid and then the other. He turned back the covers and listened to the heart. He pressed his fingers here and there on the body. He went to the end of the bed and studied the chart. He noted the time, scribbled on the chart, and then he considered the mother and the father.

This doctor was a handsome man. His skin was moist and tan. He wore a three-piece suit, a vivid tie, and on his shirt were cufflinks.

The mother was talking to herself like this. He has just come from somewhere with an audience. They gave him a special medal.

The doctor said, 'Nothing to shout about, but nothing to worry about. He should wake up pretty soon.' The doctor looked at the boy again. 'We'll know more after the tests are in.'

'Oh, no,' the mother said.

The doctor said, 'Sometimes you see this.'

The father said, 'You wouldn't call this a coma, then?'

The father waited and looked at the doctor.

'No, I don't want to call it that,' the doctor said. 'He's sleeping. It's restorative. The body is doing what it has to do.'

'It's a coma,' the mother said. 'A kind of coma.'

The doctor said, 'I wouldn't call it that.'

He took the woman's hands and patted them. He shook hands with the husband.

The woman put her fingers on the child's forehead and kept them there for a while. 'At least he doesn't have a fever,' she said. Then she said, 'I don't know. Feel his head.'

The man put his fingers on the boy's forehead. The man said, 'I think he's supposed to feel this way.'

The woman stood there awhile longer, working her lip with her teeth. Then she moved to her chair and sat down.

The husband sat in the chair beside her. He wanted to say something else. But there was no saying what it should be. He took her hand and put it in his lap. This made him feel better. It made him feel he was saying something. They sat like that for a while, watching the boy, not talking. From time to time he squeezed her hand until she took it away.

'I've been praying,' she said.

'Me too,' the father said. 'I've been praying too.'

A nurse came back in and checked the flow from the bottle.

A doctor came in and said what his name was. This doctor was wearing loafers.

'We're going to take him downstairs for more pictures,' he said. 'And we want to do a scan.'

'A scan?' the mother said. She stood between this new doctor and the bed.

'It's nothing,' he said.

'My God,' she said.

Two orderlies came in. They wheeled a thing like a bed. They unhooked the boy from the tube and slid him over onto the thing with wheels.

It was after sunup when they brought the birthday boy back out. The mother and father followed the orderlies into the elevator and up to the room. Once more the parents took up their places next to the bed.

They waited all day. The boy did not wake up. The doctor came again and examined the boy again and left after saying the same things again. Nurses came in. Doctors came in. A technician came in and took blood.

'I don't understand this,' the mother said to the technician.

'Doctor's orders,' the technician said.

The mother went to the window and looked out at the parking lot. Cars with their lights on were driving in and out. She stood at the window with her hands on the sill. She was talking to herself like this. We're into something now, something hard.

She was afraid.

She saw a car stop and a woman in a long coat get into it. She made believe she was that woman. She made believe she was driving away from here to someplace else.

The doctor came in. He looked tanned and healthier than ever. He went to the bed and examined the boy. He said, 'His signs are fine. Everything's good.'

The mother said, 'But he's sleeping.'

'Yes,' the doctor said.

The husband said, 'She's tired. She's starved.'

The doctor said, 'She should rest. She should eat. Ann,' the doctor said.

'Thank you,' the husband said.

He shook hands with the doctor and the doctor patted their shoulders and left.

'I suppose one of us should go home and check on things,' the man said. 'The dog needs to be fed.'

'Call the neighbors,' the wife said. 'Someone will feed him if you ask them to.'

She tried to think who. She closed her eyes and tried to think anything at all. After a time she said, 'Maybe I'll do it. Maybe if I'm not here watching, he'll wake up. Maybe it's because I'm watching that he won't.'

'That could be it,' the husband said.

'I'll go home and take a bath and put on something clean,' the woman said.

'I think you should do that,' the man said.

She picked up her purse. He helped her into her coat. She moved to the door, and looked back. She looked at the child, and then she looked at the father. The husband nodded and smiled.

She went past the nurses' station and down to the end of the corridor, where she turned and saw a little waiting room, a family in there, all sitting in wicker chairs, a man in a khaki shirt, a baseball cap pushed back on his head, a large woman wearing a housedress, slippers, a girl in jeans, hair in dozens of kinky braids, the table littered with flimsy wrappers and styrofoam* and coffee sticks and packets of salt and pepper.

'Nelson,' the woman said. 'Is it about Nelson?'

The woman's eyes widened.

'Tell me now, lady,' the woman said. 'Is it about Nelson?'

The woman was trying to get up from her chair. But the man had his hand closed over her arm.

'Here, here,' the man said.

'I'm sorry,' the mother said. 'I'm looking for the elevator. My son is in the hospital. I can't find the elevator.'

'Elevator is down that way,' the man said, and he aimed a finger in the right direction.

'My son was hit by a car,' the mother said. 'But he's going to be all right. He's in shock now, but it might be some kind of coma too. That's what worries us, the coma part. I'm going out for a little while. Maybe I'll take a bath. But my husband is with him. He's watching. There's a chance everything will change when I'm gone. My name is Ann Weiss.'

The man shifted in his chair. He shook his head.

He said, 'Our Nelson.'

She pulled into the driveway. The dog ran out from behind the house. He ran in circles on the grass. She closed her eyes and leaned her head against the wheel. She listened to the ticking of the engine.

She got out of the car and went to the door. She turned on lights and put on water for tea. She opened a can and fed the dog. She sat down on the sofa with her tea.

The telephone rang.

'Yes!' she said. 'Hello!' she said.

'Mrs Weiss,' a man's voice said.

'Yes,' she said. 'This is Mrs Weiss. Is it about Scotty?' she said.

'Scotty,' the voice said. 'It is about Scotty,' the voice said. 'It has to do with Scotty, yes.'

NOTES

don't hand me that (p93)
(*United States*) don't try and use that excuse or explanation
styrofoam (p97)
a kind of plastic material used for making disposable food wrappers and plastic cups

DISCUSSION

1   Why do you think the story is called *The Bath*? What significance does the actual bath have in the story? Think of some different titles for the story, and say why you think they would be less, or more, appropriate.

2   Who do you think makes the phone call at the end of the story? What effect does this phone call have? Explain what might be going through the minds of each speaker.

3   At the end of the story the reader is left hanging in mid-air, in mid-crisis. Do you find this an unsatisfactory ending? Why, or why not?

LANGUAGE FOCUS

1   Can you give a British English equivalent to these American words or phrases?

>   *potato chips* (p91), *tub* (p93), *loafers* (p96), *sunup* (p96), *elevator* (p96), *parking lot* (p96), *someplace else* (p96), *purse* (p97).

2   Throughout the story the main characters are nearly always referred to as *the mother/the woman, the boy/the child, the husband/the father/the man*. We never learn the father's name and the names Scotty and Ann Weiss are used hardly at all. What is the effect of this continual use of the definite article? Would the effect be different if names or possessive adjectives were used (e.g. *her* husband, *his* wife, *their* child)? Rewrite two or three paragraphs making these changes, and compare your version with the original.

3   The story is written in a simple, plain style with very few adjectives or images. Sometimes the sentence patterns are very repetitive and might, in another context, be called boring. Look at this extract from the end of the story:

> *... She closed her eyes and leaned her head against the wheel. She*
> *listened to the ticking of the engine.*
>
> *She got out of the car and went to the door. She turned on lights*
> *and put on water for tea. She opened a can and fed the dog. She*
> *sat down on the sofa with her tea.*

Here the pattern *she (did)* is repeated again and again. What do you
think the author is trying to suggest? Is the language itself representing
something? Try rewriting this or a similar passage in longer, more
complex sentences and using adjectives. Is the effect the same?

ACTIVITIES

1   Imagine that the boy dies, and that the driver who knocked him down
    does not come forward. Write a short report of the accident for the
    local newspaper.

2   Would you like a more definite ending? Decide how you want the
    story to end, and write a final extra paragraph. Try to follow the
    author's style, using simple sentences, *the mother, the child*, and so
    on.

3   Imagine that the boy recovers. Write a letter from the mother to her
    best friend, telling her about the accident and Scotty's recovery.

IDEAS FOR COMPARISON ACTIVITIES

1   In the stories *They Gave her a Rise* and *The Bath*, parents are afraid
    that their child might die or be dead. How are these stories different
    in their treatment of emotion and suspense? For example, how do
    we learn what the characters are feeling? Write a short paragraph to
    summarize each story, describing the differences.

2   Did you find either story moving? Why? Which story did you prefer?

SAME TIME, SAME PLACE

THE AUTHOR

Herbert Ernest Bates was born in 1905. He began his working life as a journalist, but he made his reputation as a writer with his stories about English country life. *The Darling Buds of May*, the first of the Larkin family novels, has been a popular television series. He also drew on his wartime experiences in the Royal Air Force for much of his earlier writing, which includes the novels *Fair Stood the Wind for France* and *The Jacaranda Tree*. He was one of the greatest exponents of the short-story form, with an exceptional talent for portraying character sensitively and economically. Some well-known collections of his short stories are *The Flying Goat*, *How Sleep the Brave*, *The Wedding Party*, and *The Wild Cherry Tree*. He died in 1974.

THE STORY

'The earth is a beehive; we all enter by the same door but live in different cells,' says an African proverb. That may be true, but being alone is not the same as being lonely. Some people seem content to live alone in their cell; others need the companionship of families or friends, and see their cell as a prison or a cage. And old age or poverty can make a cell even lonelier.

Miss Treadwell lives alone, in a room which is very like a real cell. She is nearing sixty, and her daily life is a series of small battles against the enemy poverty. For though Miss Treadwell is very poor indeed, it is terribly important that the rest of the world should never know it . . .

SAME TIME, SAME PLACE

One had to keep up appearances, Miss Treadwell always told herself. Whatever else happened one simply had to keep up appearances. After all one had one's pride.

The sepia musquash coat she always wore throughout the winter had not only the advantage of keeping her warm and making her look almost of upper middle class but of also concealing the fact that underneath it she wore a man's woollen cardigan and a brown imitation leather waistcoat picked up for a shilling at a rummage sale*. Underneath these garments her corsets had so far fallen to pieces that every now and then she padded them with folds of newspaper. If these failed to give her buxom but not too ample figure the distinguished and elegant line she saw so often in advertisements they at least were warm too and cheap and comforting. Above all they helped to keep up appearances.

Miss Treadwell, who was in her late fifties, was apt to refer to her minute bed-sitter, a mere dog kennel seven feet by ten*, as 'my little domain', though if occasion demanded she might enlarge a little on that, calling it 'my apartment'. A divan bed, a chair, a table and a sink left no room whatever for a cooker, though this hardly mattered, since she never cooked except to make toast over a gas-ring. Her diet consisted mostly, except on Sundays, of bread, margarine and tea, though even this, for various reasons, she only had occasionally at home.

Every morning, at about eleven o'clock, she went out and sat on one of the seats in the public gardens. One didn't have to wait long there before someone dropped a newspaper into a litter basket, so that one got the news of the day for nothing besides a new padding for the corsets when necessary. After reading for another half hour Miss Treadwell then went into a small café

round the corner and had her lunch. This too consisted of a bread
roll, margarine and a pot of tea.

It was most important always to order a pot of tea, since in this
way one got a small basin of cube sugar, most of which was easily
slipped into a handbag. It was also important to select a table
where someone else had recently been eating. In this way one quite
often found two or three pennies or even sixpence left under a
plate and uncollected by a busy waitress.

After lunch she always went back to the gardens to visit the
*Public Ladies**. It was quite extraordinary what one sometimes
found in the *Public Ladies*. Frequently someone had forgotten a
lipstick, a powder compact, a comb, a box of eye-shadow. Once
Miss Treadwell had actually found a small handbag containing,
among other things, a bottle of peroxide. With the use of this she
suddenly went sensationally and almost youthfully blonde, thus
keeping up appearances dramatically.

She had learnt other tricks by experience: for example that late
on Saturday afternoons one could buy, for a few pence, bags of
unsold cakes that wouldn't keep in the shops until Monday, or bags
of broken biscuits which made a delicious Sunday treat if you put
them in a basin and poured a layer of thin hot chocolate over them.
There were also flowers: sometimes as you walked through the
street market you came across a whole box of them, daffodils or
roses or carnations or gladioli, that had dropped from a lorry and
nobody had ever bothered to pick up. A few swiftly snatched up
stalks turned the kennel-like bed-sitter into a little paradise.

Soon after the incident of the peroxide, that had turned her a
light youthful blonde and helped to keep up her appearances so
dramatically, she was sitting in the public gardens on an April
morning. The day was suddenly and unusually hot; tulips that had
been mere half-green buds the day before were now becoming,
every moment, more and more like shimmering open wine glasses

of pink and scarlet and yellow; an occasional white or yellow
butterfly skimmed through the many wide yellow trumpets of
daffodils under trembling pink canopies of cherry blossom. All
the many seats in the gardens were crowded. It was very much a
morning when appearances mattered.

The only place she could find to sit down was next to a
gentleman who, because of the sudden April heat, had taken off
his black homburg hat and laid it on the seat beside him. As Miss
Treadwell approached he removed the hat and balanced it on his
knee. His hair was a smooth iron grey. This alone would not have
confirmed him as a gentleman but the homburg hat most certainly
did. Men who wore homburg hats were always gentlemen.

After studying his newspaper in concentrated silence for
another five minutes he folded it up and laid that too on the seat
beside him. Unwilling to appear too eager Miss Treadwell waited
some further minutes before saying:

'I hope you won't think me rude but I wonder – could I take a
tiny glance at your newspaper? I couldn't get one this morning.'

'Oh! By all means. By all means. Take it, please. I've finished
with it anyway.'

'Oh! I didn't mean to take it altogether.'

'Oh! Do. I've finished the cross-word. And once I've finished
that I'm not interested. Do you do the cross-word?'

No, Miss Treadwell had to confess, she never did the
cross-word. She supposed she wasn't clever enough for that.

'Nor was I, this morning. There was a devil of a clue and the
only word that fitted was *poitivene*. Had me stuck for an hour.
Do you know what a *poitivene* is?'

Miss Treadwell suddenly felt flattered and very pleased with
herself. Yes, she said, as a matter of fact she did.

'And what on earth is it?'

'It's a sort of chrysanthemum.'

'Is it by Jove*? How ever did you know?'

Miss Treadwell said she had seen them on the market flower stalls, named. There was another one called *rayonante*. She always thought they were such pretty names, she said, and the gentleman in the homburg hat gave her a long friendly blue-eyed stare of admiration.

Silence came between them for some few minutes after this, until finally the gentleman in the homburg hat said:

'What a beautiful morning.'

'Lovely. Spring at last.'

'Spring at last.'

Miss Treadwell now opened the paper and pretended to read it without actually seeing a single word. At the same time the gentleman in the homburg hat extended a hand and laid it on the paper and said:

'The cartoon's rather good today. Page five. Allow me.'

As the gentleman in the homburg hat turned the pages of the paper over Miss Treadwell suddenly noticed an extraordinary thing. On the third finger of his left hand he was wearing a rather large ring. It was in the shape of a turquoise butterfly set in a clear white stone.

With considerable diffidence Miss Treadwell said:

'What a most unusual ring, if you forgive me for saying so.'

'It is rather unusual.'

The gentleman in the homburg hat held out the ring for her to look at more closely. She gazed at it for some seconds and then said:

'It looks sort of Chinese.'

'Indian, I'm told.'

'Is it a sort of charm, a good luck thing or something?'

'Sort of. The butterfly is supposed to represent summer and the white stone winter and ice and all that. I suppose it's a sort of symbol of the resurgence of spring over winter. Well, so I've been told.'

Miss Treadwell could only listen in fervent, silent admiration. The stone flashed in the sun. And was it sort of lucky? she said.

'Supposed to be. But I'm afraid this thing has produced more than its fair share of trouble.'

'Oh! how could that be?'

'It belonged to my eldest sister. She left it to me. Consequently my other sister – I live with her – has never forgiven her. She gives me hell about it.'

Miss Treadwell fell into a depressive silence, not knowing what to say. The silence lasted several minutes until at last he said:

'Still, I suppose I ought to be thankful she looks after me. Do you live near by?'

'My apartment is just round the corner.'

'You live alone?'

'Oh! quite.'

'In a way I envy you. At least you've no one to quarrel with. Every day I'm glad when breakfast is over. Then I can be off on my own.'

In silence Miss Treadwell again gazed at the butterfly imprisoned in its ice.

'Do you find it difficult to fill in the day?' the man in the homburg hat said.

'Oh! no, no, no. It's terribly, terribly full. By the time I've done my cooking and cleared up the apartment and so on the time simply flies. I do a lot of flower arrangement.'

'I find it hangs like hell.'

They sat for some time longer in the sun, without speaking. Then the man in the homburg hat looked at his pocket watch and said:

'Well, I fear I must be going: we always have lunch at dead on twelve. If I'm not there she starts creating like fury*.'

'I must be going too,' Miss Treadwell said. 'I've my own lunch to get. And then I'm making new curtains for the sitting-room.'

'Ah! you're clever at that sort of thing?'

'Oh! I don't know about clever. As a matter of fact I don't think I am. I sort of mis-measured the windows and now I need yards and yards more material.'

'I suppose that's the trouble with large windows.'

'Yes. Yes. However, we shall get over it. I know they have plenty more at the shop.'

The man in the homburg hat got up, put on his hat and then took it off again in a courteous gesture.

'Well, goodbye. It's been so nice to meet you. Oh! by the way my name is Thornhill.'

The butterfly imprisoned in its ice flashed in the sun.

'And you, Mr Thornhill.'

After that they began to meet at more or less the same spot, at more or less the same time, on most weekdays. The weather continued warm, sometimes even hot, and Miss Treadwell discarded the musquash coat and some of the newspaper under it, wearing instead a pale pink jersey dress and a pair of brown imitation crocodile shoes she had picked up for a shilling or two at a rummage sale.

'I'm feeling rather affluent today,' was the first remark with which Mr Thornhill greeted Miss Treadwell one morning. They had been meeting for nearly a month now.

'Oh? Why is that?'

'I've started to draw my pension*.' He laughed, rather against himself, pleasantly. 'I think it's rather funny. Do you have the pension yet?'

Oh! no, no, dear me no, Miss Treadwell said. She laughed too. Did he mind? She hadn't quite got as far as that yet. All in good time.

'Earlier in life one tends to rather despise the thought. And when the time comes it's rather nice. Well, I expect you won't be too proud to take it when it arrives?'

'Well, of course luckily I have private means.' It was a lie, but one had to keep up appearances. Miss Treadwell's means consisted of a small Post Office Savings Account from which she extracted a minute sum every Monday morning. 'I simply couldn't manage the apartment without.'

'Those curtains must have cost you a bit.'

'Oh! the earth. The absolute earth.'

'On the subject of affluence,' he suddenly said, 'I feel in honour bound to buy you a drink this morning. Would you?'

'But it's only half past eleven—'

'By the time we've walked to *The Lansdowne Arms** it'll be twelve o'clock.'

'*The Lansdowne Arms*—'

Miss Treadwell, who couldn't afford to drink anyway, suddenly found herself confronted with impossible visions of grandeur and felt slightly frightened. Walking across the public gardens she kept her hands tightly folded in front of her, in case one or more of the newspapers should slip and fall down.

In the bar of *The Lansdowne Arms* all was wrapped in a red, subdued light. Like scarlet torches a great vase of gladioli flamed on the bar.

'Now name it,' Mr Thornhill said. 'Anything you like. After all it isn't every day a man becomes of age. Sherry, port, gin, whisky, beer? – what shall it be?'

Miss Treadwell hesitatingly confessed that she felt ever so slightly tempted towards a small sherry.

'Splendid. I'll have a sherry too. But a dry one. And make them,' he said to the waiting barman, 'large ones.'

Sherry in hand, Miss Treadwell sat bathed in dreams of grandeur that, for all their emergence into reality, were now more impossible than ever. The sherry warmed her throat, crawled snakily through her empty stomach and moistened her eyes. Mr Thornhill said 'cheers' several times and then suddenly burst out laughing.

'God, I wish my sister could see me now.'

He positively swigged at his sherry while Miss Treadwell gently sipped at hers.

'Hell. Why do the children of the same parents so often hate each other?'

To this question, almost barked out, Miss Treadwell had no answer and simply went on sipping her sherry.

'Some days the atmosphere in that house is poisonous. We hiss at each other like two snakes. One day—'

Miss Treadwell started to think up what seemed at first a presumptuous remark but another sip or two of sherry finally fortified her to make it.

'Perhaps if you gave her the ring it might help things—'

'Good God, what? Can't you just hear her? – "Oh! far be it from me to take the ring from you. If Alice had wished me to have the ring she would have left it to me. But the fact is she didn't, did she? Oh! no it's your ring. Not all the wild dogs in China" – that's one of her favourite maddening expressions, "all the wild dogs in China" –'

Mr Thornhill savagely drained his sherry glass.

'Have you ever known what it is to want to murder somebody?'

Oh! dear me no, Miss Treadwell said, her voice barely audible. Oh! dear me—

'It's not funny.' Mr Thornhill said. 'It's not funny. Still, drink up. Second round. This is the day.'

Miss Treadwell started meekly to protest that really one was enough for her, but Mr Thornhill was already waving an expansive arm in the direction of the bar.

'Well, if you insist,' Miss Treadwell said, 'but only a very small one this time—'

Of course he insisted, Mr Thornhill said and snapped out the words 'Same again, barman,' only to retract them a second later.

'No, make mine whisky. A double Black-and-White.'

His sister didn't drink either, he went on to say. That made her sub-human for a start. A good drink now and then did a lot to make a person human, didn't Miss Treadwell agree?

The barman having brought the new drinks Mr Thornhill drank gaspily at his whisky, confessing that sherry really wasn't his tipple. With whisky a man had something. It – what did they say nowadays? – it sent you.

'We must do this more often. Make it an every morning thing.'

Mr Thornhill, having drunk half his whisky neat, now poured a little water into the rest of it, complaining at the same time that you didn't get much of a measure nowadays. In no time you were ready for another.

'By the way, did you finish your curtains?'

No, Miss Treadwell had to confess, she hadn't yet.

'Well, promise me something. When you do, invite me up to see them. Fair enough? I envy you that apartment of yours. I really envy you. God, it would be nice to live on one's own – Well, promise me?'

Well, it would be some time yet, Miss Treadwell found herself saying. Inwardly she trembled with cold apprehension. There had been some hitch about the material. The stock of the original yellow had run out and she hadn't been able to match it up.

'Well, all in good time. All in good time. But promise me?'

After a third large whisky Mr Thornhill gave the distinct

impression of talking through a muslin bag. The folds of his neck were perceptibly reddened. From time to time he locked and unlocked the fingers of his two hands and finally, in one of these unsteady gestures, he took off the butterfly ring. To her infinite and tortured astonishment Miss Treadwell suddenly heard the words:

'You said something about giving the ring back to Beryl. Well, blast Beryl. I want to give it to you. Get what I mean?' He held out the bright imprisoned butterfly. 'Go on. Take it. Slip it on.'

'Mr Thornhill, I don't quite understand—'

'Go on. Third finger, left hand.'

The butterfly imprisoned in its ice sparkled. Miss Treadwell proceeded to lift her glass of sherry, only to find herself trembling so much that she had to set it down again. Mr Thornhill smacked the palms of his hands together and his voice was over-loud.

'You get what I'm asking you, don't you? It isn't always easy to say these things.'

Half-terrified, Miss Treadwell made yet another attempt to lift her glass of sherry. This time she managed to get it to her lips, spilling much of it down her chin. As she mopped at it with her handkerchief it appeared to Mr Thornhill that she might have been about to cry. She did in fact feel like crying and sat for some moments biting her lips hard, locked in impotent nervous distress.

'Well,' Mr Thornhill said. 'What say you? Do you know, I don't even know your Christian name.'

'Doris.'

Mr Thornhill laughed tipsily.

'Doris, I'm asking you – yes I know – I expect you're going to say "this is all so sudden"—'

Well, it was, sort of, Miss Treadwell said. A vision of her bed-sitter, the dog-kennel, suddenly rose up to mock her. The loud plop of the gas-ring as she lit it echoed through her mind, extinguishing for a moment every thought. Again the imprisoned butterfly sparkled. A moment later, unsteadily grabbing at his glass, Mr Thornhill dropped the ring on the floor.

Picking it up, he was visibly trembling too.

'I thought perhaps we could both manage in your apartment with my pension and your – unless perhaps you'd prefer to be independent—'

Desperately, as never before in her life, Miss Treadwell sought to keep up appearances by taking her powder compact from her bag, looking into its mirror and slowly powdering her nose. The face she saw in the glass, pallid and stiff, seemed not to belong to her and hastily she shut the compact down.

'Well, what do you say?'

'I don't know what – well, anyway not today, Mr Thornhill. Please, not today.'

'Not Mister Thornhill. Harry. Tomorrow then? Same time, same place, tomorrow. Here.'

'I think I ought to go now, Mr Thornhill.'

'Harry, Harry please. Go, my foot. I'm going to have another whisky.' Mr Thornhill's command of 'Same again' was so sharp and loud that a wire-haired terrier belonging to a tweeded gentleman at the far end of the bar yapped out a series of loud and agitated barks. In its feverish agitation it might well have been the echo of the voice of Miss Treadwell pleading for some sort of escape or mercy.

'Goodbye,' she said. 'I really must go.' Her voice was in fact barely audible. 'Goodbye – I really must go now—'

'Don't forget.' Mr Thornhill staggered unsteadily to his feet, eyes watering weakly, the imprisoned butterfly flashing again as he sought to shake her hand. 'Same time, same place—'

After that Miss Treadwell never sat in the public gardens again. She now goes, instead, to a park half a mile away. In the park is a small lake. In the centre of the lake is an island covered with low shrubbery and a number of wooden coops where ornamental water-birds, bright mallards, unusual geese and even moorhens can shelter.

Every morning Miss Treadwell, struggling always, with pride, to keep up appearances, takes with her a small bag of stale cakes or broken biscuits and throws them to the birds and then persuades herself it is sort of fun to watch which ones, greedy and squabbling, grab the biggest pieces first.

'Tomorrow,' she always tells herself. 'Same time, same place.'

She also reads the newspaper.

NOTES

rummage sale (p103)
(*United States*) a jumble sale, a sale of old unwanted goods (often secondhand clothes) to raise money for charity

seven feet by ten (p103)
about two metres by three metres

Public Ladies (p104)
ladies' public toilets

by Jove (p106)
(*dated informal*) an exclamation to express surprise (Jove was an ancient Roman god)

creating like fury (p108)
(*informal*) getting very angry, making a terrible fuss

pension (p108)
a sum of money paid regularly by the State to certain people; here, the pension would be the old age pension paid to men at the age of 65, and women at the age of 60

The Lansdowne Arms (p109)
the name of a local pub (public house)

DISCUSSION

1 Describe the ways in which Miss Treadwell keeps up appearances. Why do you think she feels it is important to do this?

2 Miss Treadwell and Mr Thornhill are both shown as rather pathetic figures. Do you think either of them is lonely? Who do you feel more sympathy for? Why?

3 Why do you think Miss Treadwell does not accept Mr Thornhill's proposal? Is it because of shame, pride, fear, dislike or some other reason? Do you think she would have accepted him if he had known her true circumstances? Or indeed, if he had known them, would he have proposed marriage in the first place?

LANGUAGE FOCUS

1 What words and expressions does Miss Treadwell use to give the impression to Mr Thornhill that she is quite well-off? Make a list of

them. How many of these are direct untruths, and how many are open to misinterpretation, and so become untruthful only because of the way Mr Thornhill interprets them?

2   Mr Thornhill's ring is mentioned several times during the story – 'the butterfly imprisoned in ice'. Mr Thornhill explains it is a 'symbol of the resurgence of spring over winter'. What else in the story do you think it could symbolize?

ACTIVITIES

1   Imagine that Miss Treadwell and Mr Thornhill meet by chance a year after the story. What do they say to each other? Write their dialogue.

2   Suppose Miss Treadwell had accepted Mr Thornhill's proposal. Write a new ending for the story. What does Mr Thornhill's sister do? Do Mr Thornhill and Miss Treadwell live happily ever after, or does the story have a tragic ending?

A Bit of Singing
and Dancing

The Author

Susan Hill was born in Scarborough in 1942. She is a
novelist, playwright, and critic, who has also written several
radio plays and broadcasts frequently. Some of her novels
are *I'm the King of the Castle, Strange Meeting, The Bird
of Night. The Albatross* and *A Bit of Singing and Dancing*
are both collections of short stories. Most of her novels and
short stories are about difficult emotional relationships, but
she writes with delicacy and compassion.

The Story

Tyranny can take many forms: the tyranny of rulers over
people, the tyranny of one individual over another, the
tyranny of unjust imprisonment, military force, psycho-
logical or emotional domination. Most people want to
escape from tyranny of any kind – to be free, free to make
their own choices, their own decisions. But when you are
not used to it, freedom can be difficult to live with. 'Liberty
is a different kind of pain from prison,' wrote T.S. Eliot in
his play *The Family Reunion*.

Esme Fanshaw has suddenly been released into
longed-for liberty by the death of her tyrannical mother.
Now she can do, say, think what she likes. She can please
herself about everything and anything; the choices are
endless – and bewildering. It is not easy to shake off fifty
years of domination . . .

A BIT OF SINGING AND DANCING

There was no one else on the beach so late in the afternoon. She walked very close to the water, where there was a rim of hard, flat sand, easier on her feet than the loose shelves of shingle, which folded one on top of the other, up to the storm wall. She thought, I can stay out here just as long as I like. I can do anything I choose, anything at all, for now I am answerable only to myself.

But it was an unpromising afternoon, already half dark, an afternoon for early tea and banked-up fires and entertainment on television. And a small thrill went through her as she realized that that, too, was entirely up to her, she could watch whichever programme she chose, or not watch any at all. There had not been an evening for the past eleven years when the television had stayed off and there was silence to hear the ticking of the clock and the central heating pipes.

'It is her only pleasure,' she used to say, 'She sees things she would otherwise be quite unable to see, the television has given her a new lease of life. You're never too old to learn.' But in truth her mother had watched variety shows, Morecambe and Wise and the Black and White Minstrels*, whereas she herself would have chosen BBC 2* and something cultural or educational.

'I like a bit of singing and dancing, it cheers you up, Esme, it takes you out of yourself. I like a bit of spectacular.'

But tonight there might be a play or a film about Arabia or the Archipelagoes, or a master class for cellists, tonight she would please herself for the first time. Because it was two weeks now, since her mother's death, a decent interval.

It was February. It was a cold evening. As far as she could see, the beach and the sea and the sky were all grey, merging into one another in the distance. On the day of her mother's funeral it had been blowing a gale, with sleet, she had looked round at all their lifeless, pinched faces under the black hats and thought, this is right, this is fitting, that we should all of us seem bowed and old and disconsolate. Her mother had a right to a proper grief, a proper mourning.

She had wanted to leave the beach and walk back, her hands were stiff with cold inside the pockets of her navy-blue coat – navy, she thought, was the correct first step away from black. She wanted to go back and toast scones and eat them with too much butter, of which her mother would have strongly disapproved. 'We never had it, *we* were never allowed to indulge ourselves in rich foods, and besides, they've been discovering more about heart disease in relation to butter, haven't you read that in the newspapers, Esme? I'm surprised you don't pay attention to these things. I pay attention. I don't believe in butter at every meal – butter on this, butter with that.'

Every morning her mother had read two newspapers from cover to cover – the *Daily Telegraph** and the *Daily Mirror**, and marked out with a green ball point pen news items in which she thought that her daughter ought to take an interest. She said, 'I like to see both sides of every question.' And so, whichever side her daughter or some visitor took, on some issue of the day, she was informed enough by both her newspapers to take the opposing view. An argument, she had said, sharpened the mind.

'I do not intend to become a cabbage, Esme, just because I am forced to be bedridden.'

She had reached the breakwater. A few gulls circled, bleating, in the gunmetal sky, and the waterline was strewn with fishheads, the flesh all picked away. She thought, I am free, I may go on or go back, or else stand here for an hour, I am mistress of myself. It was a long time since she had been out for so long, she could not quite get used to it, this absence of the need to look at her watch, to scurry home. But after a while, because it was really very damp and there was so little to see, she did turn, and then the thought of tomorrow, and the outing she had promised herself to buy new clothes. It would take some months for her mother's will to be proven, the solicitor had explained to her, things were generally delayed, but there was no doubt that they would be settled to her advantage and really, Mrs Fanshaw had been very careful, very prudent, and so she would not be in want. Meanwhile, perhaps an advance for immediate expenses? Perhaps a hundred pounds?

When the will was read, her first reaction had been one of admiration, she had said, 'The cunning old woman' under her breath, and then put her hand up to her mouth, afraid of being overheard. 'The cunning old woman.' For Mildred Fanshaw had saved up £6,000, scattered about in bank and savings accounts. Yet they had always apparently depended upon Esme's salary and the old age pension, they had had to be careful, she said, about electricity and extra cream and joints of beef. 'Extravagance,' Mrs Fanshaw said, 'it is a cardinal sin. That is where all other evils stem from, Esme. Extravagance. We should all live within our means.'

And now here was £6,000. For a moment or two it had gone to her head, she had been quite giddy with plans, she would buy a car and learn to drive, buy a washing machine and a television set, she would have a holiday abroad and get properly fitting underwear and eat out in a restaurant now and again, she would . . .

But she was over fifty, she should be putting money on one side herself now, saving for her own old age, and besides, even the idea of spending made her feel guilty, as though her mother could hear, now, what was going on inside her head, just as, in life, she had known her thoughts from the expression on her face.

She had reached the steps leading up from the beach. It was almost dark.

She shivered, then, in a moment of fear and bewilderment at her new freedom, for there was nothing she had to do, she could please herself about everything, anything, and this she could not get used to. Perhaps she ought not to stay here, perhaps she could try and sell the house, which was really far too big for her, perhaps she ought to get a job and a small flat in London. London was the city of opportunity . . .

She felt flushed and a little drunk then, she felt that all things were possible, the future was in her power, and she wanted to shout and sing and dance, standing alone in the February twilight, looking at the deserted beach. All the houses along the seafront promenade had blank, black windows, for this was a summer place, in February it was only half alive.

She said, 'And that is what I have been. But I am fifty-one years old and look at the chances before me.'

Far out on the shingle bank the green warning light flashed on-on-off, on-on-off. It had been flashing the night of her mother's stroke, she had gone to the window and watched it and felt comforted at three a.m. in the aftermath of death. Now, the shock of that death came to her again like a hand slapped across her face, she thought, my mother is not here, my mother is in a box in the earth, and she began to shiver violently, her mind crawling with images of corruption, she started to walk very quickly along the promenade and up the hill towards home.

When she opened the front door she listened, and everything was quite silent, quite still. There had always been the voice from upstairs, 'Esme?' and each time she had wanted to say, 'Who else would it be?' and bitten back the words, only said, 'Hello, it's me.' Now, again, she called, 'It's me. Hello,' and her voice echoed softly up the dark stair well, when she heard it, it was a shock, for what kind of woman was it who talked to herself and was afraid of an empty house? What kind of woman?

She went quickly into the sitting-room and drew the curtains and then poured herself a small glass of sherry, the kind her mother had preferred. It was shock, of course, they had told her, all of them, her brother-in-law and her Uncle Cecil and cousin George Golightly, when they had come back for tea and ham sandwiches after the funeral.

'You will feel the real shock later. Shock is always delayed.' Because she had been so calm and self-possessed, she had made all the arrangements so neatly, they were very surprised.

'If you ever feel the need of company, Esme – and you will – of course you must come to us. Just a telephone call, that's all we need, just a little warning in advance. You are sure to feel strange.'

Strange. Yes. She sat by the electric fire. Well, the truth was she had got herself thoroughly chilled, walking on the beach like that, so late in the afternoon. It had been her own fault.

After a while, the silence of the house oppressed her, so that when she had taken a second glass of sherry and made herself a poached egg on toast, she turned on the television and watched a variety show, because it was something cheerful, and she needed taking out of herself. There would be time enough for the educational programmes when she was used to this new life. But a thought went through her head, backwards and forwards, backwards and forwards, it was as though she were reading from a tape.

'She is upstairs. She is still in her room. If you go upstairs you will see her. Your mother.' The words danced across the television screen, intermingling with the limbs of dancers, issuing like spume out of the mouths of comedians and crooners, they took on the rhythm of the drums and the double basses.

'Upstairs. In her room. Upstairs. In her room.

Your mother. Your mother. Your mother.

Upstairs . . .'

She jabbed at the push button on top of the set and the pictures shrank and died, there was silence, and then she heard her own heart beating and the breath coming out of her in little gasps. She scolded herself for being morbid, neurotic. Very well then, she said, go upstairs and see for yourself.

Very deliberately and calmly she went out of the room and climbed the stairs, and went into her mother's bedroom. The light from the street lamp immediately outside the window shone a pale triangle of light down onto the white runner on the dressing table, the white lining of the curtains and the smooth white cover of the bed. Everything had gone. Her mother might never have been here. Esme had been very anxious not to hoard reminders and so, the very day after the funeral, she had cleared out and packed up clothes, linen, medicine, papers, spectacles, she had ruthlessly emptied the room of her mother.

Now, standing in the doorway, smelling lavender polish and dust, she felt ashamed, as though she wanted to be rid of all memory, as though she had wanted her mother to die. She said, but that is what I did want, to be rid of the person who bound me to her for fifty years. She spoke aloud into the bedroom, 'I wanted you dead.' She felt her hands trembling and held them tightly together, she thought, I am a wicked woman. But the sherry she had drunk began to have some effect now, her heart was beating more quietly, and she was able to walk out into the room and draw the curtains, even though it was now unnecessary to scold herself for being so hysterical.

In the living room, she sat beside the fire reading a historical biography until eleven o'clock – when her mother was alive she had always been in bed by ten – and the fears had quite left her, she felt entirely calm. She thought, it is only natural, you have had a shock, you are bound to be affected. That night she slept extremely well.

When she answered the front doorbell at eleven fifteen the following morning and found Mr Amos Curry, hat in hand, upon the step, inquiring about a room, she remembered a remark her Uncle Cecil had made to her on the day of the funeral. 'You will surely not want to be here all on your own, Esme, in this great house. You should take a lodger.'

Mr Amos Curry rubbed his left eyebrow with a nervous finger, a gesture of his because he was habitually shy. 'A room to let,' he said, and she noticed that he wore gold cuff links and very well-polished shoes. 'I understand from the agency . . . a room to let with breakfast.'

'I know nothing of any agency. I think you have the wrong address.'

He took out a small loose-leaf notebook. 'Number 23, Park Close.'

'Oh no, I'm so sorry, we are . . .' she corrected herself, 'I am twenty-three Park *Walk*.'

A flush of embarrassment began to seep up over his face and neck like an ink stain, he loosened his collar a little until she felt quite sorry for him, quite upset.

'An easy mistake, a perfectly understandable mistake. Mr . . . Please do not feel at all . . .'

'. . . Curry. Amos Curry.'

'. . . embarrassed.'

'I am looking for a quiet room with breakfast. It seemed so hopeful. Park Close. Such a comfortable address.'

She thought, he is a very clean man, very neat and spruce, he has a gold incisor tooth and he wears gloves. Her mother had always approved of men who wore gloves. 'So few do, nowadays. Gloves and hats. It is easy to pick out a gentleman.'

Mr Curry also wore a hat.

'I do apologize, Madam, I feel so ... I would not have troubled ...'

'No ... no, please ...'

'I must look for Park Close, Number 23.'

'It is just around the bend, to the left, a few hundred yards. A very secluded road.'

'Like this. This road is secluded. I thought as I approached this house, how suitable, I should ... I feel one can tell, a house has a certain ... But I am so sorry.'

He settled his hat upon his neat grey hair, and then raised it again politely, turning away.

She took in a quick breath. She said, 'What exactly ... that is to say, if you are looking for a room with breakfast, I wonder if I ...'

Mr Amos Curry turned back.

He held a small pickled onion delicately on the end of his fork. 'There is,' he said, 'the question of my equipment.'

Esme Fanshaw heard his voice as though it issued from the wireless – there was a distortion about it, a curious echo. She shook her head. He is not real, she thought ... But he was here, Mr Amos Curry, in a navy-blue pin stripe suit and with a small neat darn just below his shirt collar. He was sitting at her kitchen table – for she had hesitated to ask him into the dining room, which in any case was rarely used, the kitchen had seemed a proper compromise. He was here. She had made a pot of coffee, and then, after an hour, a cold snack of beef and pickles, bread and butter, her hands were a little moist with excitement. She thought again how rash she had been, she said, he is a total stranger, someone from the street, a casual caller, I know nothing at all about him. But she recognized the voice of her mother, then, and rebelled against it. Besides, it was not true, for Mr Curry had told her a great deal. She thought, this is how life should be, I should be daring. I should allow myself to be constantly surprised. Each day I should be ready for some new encounter. That is how to stay young. She was most anxious to stay young.

In his youth, Mr Curry had been abroad a great deal, had lived, he said, in Ceylon, Singapore and India. 'I always keep an open mind, Miss Fanshaw, I believe in the principle of tolerance, live and let live. Nation shall speak peace unto nation.'

'Oh, I do agree.'

'I have seen the world and its ways. I have no prejudices. The customs of others may be quite different from our own but human beings are human beings the world over. We learn from one another every day. By keeping an open mind, Miss Fanshaw.'

'Oh yes.'

'You have travelled?'

'I – I have visited Europe. Not too far afield, I'm afraid.'

'I have journeyed on foot through most of the European countries, I have earned my passage at all times.'

She did not like to ask how, but she was impressed, having only been abroad once herself, to France.

Mr Curry had been an orphan, he said, life for him had begun in a children's home. 'But it was a more than adequate start, Miss Fanshaw, we were all happy together. I do not think memory deceives me. We were one big family. Never let it be said that the Society* did not do its best by me. I see how lucky I am. Well, you have only to look about you, Miss Fanshaw – how many people do you see from broken families, unhappy homes? I know nothing of that: I count myself fortunate. I like to think I have made the best of my circumstances.'

His education, he said, had been rather elementary, he had a good brain which had never been taxed to the full.

'Untapped resources,' he said, pointing to his forehead.

They talked so easily, she thought she had never found conversation flowing along with any other stranger, any other man. Mr Curry had exactly the right amount of formal politeness, mixed with informal ease, and she decided that he was destined to live here, he had style and he seemed so much at home.

He had an ordinary face, for which she was grateful, but there was something slightly unreal about it, as though she were seeing it on a cinema screen. All the same, it was very easy to picture him sitting in this kitchen, eating breakfast, before putting on his hat, which had a small feather in the band, each morning and going off to work.

'I do have some rather bulky equipment.'

'What exactly . . .'

'I have two jobs, Miss Fanshaw, two strings to my bow, as it were. That surprises you? But I have always been anxious to fill up every hour of the day, I have boundless energy.'

She noticed that he had some tufts of pepper coloured hair sprouting from his ears and nostrils and wondered if, when he visited the barber for a haircut, he also had these trimmed. She knew nothing about the habits of men.

'Of course, it is to some extent seasonal work.'

'Seasonal?'

'Yes. For those odd wet and windy days which always come upon us at the English seaside, and of course during the winter, I travel in cleaning utensils.'

He looked around him quickly, as though to see where she kept her polish and dusters and brooms, to make note of any requirements.

'Perhaps you would require some extra storage space? Other than the room itself.'

Mr Curry got up from the table and began to clear away dishes, she watched him in astonishment. The man on the doorstep with a note of the wrong address had become the luncheon visitor, the friend who helped with the washing up.

'There is quite a large loft.'

'Inaccessible.'

'Oh.'

'And I do have to be a little careful. No strain on the back. Not that I am a sick man, Miss Fanshaw, I hasten to reassure you, you will not have an invalid on your hands. Oh no. I am extremely healthy for my age. It is because I lead such an active life.'

She thought of him, knocking upon all the doors, walking back down so many front paths. Though this was not what he did in the summer.

'Sound in wind and limb, as you might say.'

She thought of racehorses, and tried to decide whether he had ever been married. She said, 'Or else, perhaps, the large cupboard under the stairs, where the gas meter . . .'

'Perfect.'

He poured just the right amount of washing up liquid into the bowl; his sleeves were already unbuttoned and rolled up to the elbows, his jacket hung on the hook behind the back door. She saw the hairs lying like thatch on his sinewy arms, and a dozen questions sprang up into her mind, then, for although he seemed to have told her a great deal about himself, there were many gaps.

He had visited the town previously, he told her, in the course of his work, and fell for it. 'I never forgot it, Miss Fanshaw. I should be very happy here, I told myself. It is my kind of place. Do you see?'

'And so you came back.'

'Certainly. I know when I am meant to do something. I never ignore that feeling. I was intended to return here.'

'It is rather a small town.'

'But select.'

'I was only wondering – we do have a very short season, really only July and August . . .'

'Yes?'

'Perhaps it would not be suitable for your – er – summer work?'

'Oh, I think it would, Miss Fanshaw, I think so, I size these things up rather carefully, you know, rather carefully.'

She did not question him further, only said, 'Well, it is winter now.'

'Indeed. I shall, to coin a phrase, be plying my other trade. In a town like this, full of ladies such as yourself, in nice houses with comfortable circumstances, the possibilities are endless, endless.'

'For – er – cleaning materials?'

'Quite so.'

'I do see that.'

'Now you take a pride, don't you? Anyone can see that for himself.'

He waved a hand around the small kitchen, scattering little drops of foamy water, and she saw the room through his eyes, the clean windows, the shining taps, the immaculate sinks. Yes, she took a pride, that was true. Her mother had insisted upon it. Now, she heard herself saying, 'My mother died only a fortnight ago,' forgetting that she had told him already and the shock of the fact overcame her again, she could not believe in the empty room, which she was planning to give to Mr Curry, and her eyes filled up with tears of guilt. And what would her mother have said about a strange man washing up in their kitchen, about this new, daring friendship.

'You should have consulted me, Esme, you take far too much on trust. You never think. You should have consulted me.'

Two days after her mother's funeral, Mrs Bickerdike, from The Lilacs, had met her in the pharmacy, and mentioned, in lowered voice, that she 'did work for the bereaved', which, Esme gathered, meant that she conducted seances. She implied that contact might be established with the deceased Mrs Fanshaw. Esme had been shocked, most of all by the thought of that contact, and a continuing relationship with her mother, though she had only said that she believed in letting the dead have their rest. 'I think, if you will forgive me, and with respect, that we are not meant to inquire about them, or to follow them on.'

Now, she heard her mother talking about Mr Curry. 'You should always take particular notice of the eyes, Esme, never trust anyone with eyes set too closely together.'

She tried to see his eyes, but he was turned sideways to her.

'Or else too widely apart. That indicates idleness.'

She was ashamed of what she had just said about her mother's recent death, for she did not at all wish to embarrass him, or to appear hysterical. Mr Curry had finished washing up and was resting his reddened wet hands upon the rim of the sink. When he spoke, his voice was a little changed and rather solemn. 'I do not believe in shutting away the dead, Miss Fanshaw, I believe in the sacredness of memory. I am only glad that you feel able to talk to me about the good lady.'

She felt suddenly glad to have him here in the kitchen, for his presence took the edge off the emptiness and silence which lately had seemed to fill up every corner of the house.

She said, 'It was not always easy . . . My mother was a very . . . forthright woman.'

'Say no more. I understand only too well. The older generation believed in speaking their minds.'

She thought, he is obviously a very sensitive man, he can read between the lines: and she wanted to laugh with relief, for there was no need to go into details about how dominating her mother had been and how taxing were the last years of her illness – he knew, he understood.

Mr Curry dried his hands, smoothing the towel down one finger at a time, as though he were drawing on gloves. He rolled down his shirt-sleeves and fastened them and put on his jacket. His movements were neat and deliberate. He coughed. 'Regarding the room – there is just the question of payment, Miss Fanshaw, I believe in having these matters out at once. There is nothing to be embarrassed about in speaking of money, I hope you agree.'

'Oh no, certainly, I . . .'

'Shall we say four pounds a week?'

Her head swam. She had no idea at all how much a lodger should pay, how much his breakfasts would cost, and she was anxious to be both business-like and fair. Well, he had suggested what seemed to him a most suitable sum, he was more experienced in these matters than herself.

'For the time being I am staying at a commercial guest house in Cedars Road. I have only linoleum covering the floor of my room, there is nothing cooked at breakfast. I am not accustomed to luxury, Miss Fanshaw, you will understand that from what I have told you of my life, but I think I am entitled to comfort at the end of the working day.'

'Oh, you will be more than comfortable here, I shall see to that, I shall do my very best. I feel . . .'

'Yes?'

She was suddenly nervous of how she appeared in his eyes.

'I do feel that the mistake you made in the address was somehow . . .'

'Fortuitous.'

'Yes, oh yes.'

Mr Curry gave a little bow.

'When would you wish to move in, Mr Curry? There are one or two things . . .'

'Tomorrow evening, say?'

'Tomorrow is Friday.'

'Perhaps that is inconvenient.'

'No . . . no . . . certainly . . . our week could begin on a Friday, as it were.'

'I shall greatly look forward to having you as a landlady, Miss Fanshaw.'

Landlady. She wanted to say, 'I hope I shall be a friend, Mr Curry,' but it sounded presumptuous.

When he had gone she made herself a pot of tea, and sat quietly at the kitchen table, a little dazed. She thought, this is a new phase of my life. But she was still a little alarmed. She had acted out of character and against what she would normally have called her better judgement. Her mother would have warned her against inviting strangers into the house, just as, when she was a child, she had warned her about speaking to them in the street. 'You can never be sure, Esme, there are some very peculiar people about.' For she was a great reader of the crime reports in her newspapers, and of books about famous trials. The life of Doctor Crippen* had particularly impressed her.

Esme shook her head. Now, all the plans she had made for selling the house and moving to London and going abroad were necessarily curtailed, and for the moment she felt depressed, as though the old life were going to continue, and she wondered, too, what neighbours and friends might say, and whether anyone had seen Mr Curry standing on her doorstep, paper in hand, whether, when he went from house to house selling cleaning utensils, they would recognize him as Miss Fanshaw's lodger and disapprove. There was no doubt that her mother would have disapproved, and not only because he was a 'stranger off the streets'.

'He is a salesman, Esme, a doorstep pedlar, and you do not *know* what his employment in the summer months may turn out to be.'

'He has impeccable manners, mother, quite old-fashioned ones, and a most genteel way of speaking.' She remembered the gloves and the raised hat, the little bow, and also the way he had quietly and confidently done the washing up, as though he were already living here.

'How do you know where things will lead, Esme?'

'I am prepared to take a risk. I have taken too few risks in my life so far.'

She saw her mother purse her lips and fold her hands together, refusing to argue further, only certain that she was in the right. Well, it was her own life now, and she was mistress of it, she would follow her instincts for once. And she went and got a sheet of paper, on which to write a list of things that were needed to make her mother's old bedroom quite comfortable for him. After that, she would buy cereal and bacon and kidneys for the week's breakfasts.

She was surprised at how little time it took for her to grow quite accustomed to having Mr Curry in the house. It helped, of course, that he was a man of very regular habits and neat, too, when she had first gone into his room to clean it, she could have believed that no one was using it at all. The bed was neatly made, clothes hung out of sight in drawers – he had locked the wardrobe, she discovered, and taken away the key. Only two pairs of shoes side by side, below the washbasin, and a shaving brush and razor on the shelf above it, gave the lodger away.

Mr Curry got up promptly at eight – she heard his alarm clock and then the pips of the radio news. At eight twenty he came down to the kitchen for his breakfast, smelling of shaving soap and shoe polish. Always, he said, 'Ah, good morning, Miss Fanshaw, good morning to you,' and then commented briefly upon the weather. It was 'a bit nippy' or 'a touch of sunshine, I see' or 'bleak'. He ate a cooked breakfast, followed by toast and two cups of strong tea.

Esme took a pride in her breakfasts, in the neat way she laid the table and the freshness of the cloth, she warmed his plate under the grill and waited until the last minute before doing the toast so that it should still be crisp and hot. She thought, it is a very bad thing for a woman such as myself to live alone and become entirely selfish. I am the sort of person who needs to give service.

At ten minutes to nine, Mr Curry got his suitcase from the downstairs cupboard, wished her good morning again, and left the house. After that she was free for the rest of the day, to live as she had always lived, or else to make changes – though much of her time was taken with cleaning the house and especially Mr Curry's room, and shopping for something unusual for Mr Curry's breakfasts.

She had hoped to enrol for lampshade-making classes at the evening institute but it was too late for that year, they had told her she must apply again after the summer, so she borrowed a book upon the subject from the public library and bought frames and card and fringing, and taught herself. She went to one or two bring-and-buy sales and planned to hold a coffee morning and do a little voluntary work for old people. Her life was full. She enjoyed having Mr Curry in the house. Easter came, and she began to wonder when he would change to his summer work, and what that work might be. He never spoke of it.

To begin with he had come in between five thirty and six every evening, and gone straight to his room. Sometimes he went out again for an hour, she presumed to buy a meal somewhere and perhaps drink a glass of beer, but more often he stayed in, and Esme did not see him again until the following morning. Once or twice she heard music coming from his room – presumably from the radio, and she thought how nice it was to hear that the house was alive, a home for someone else.

One Friday evening, Mr Curry came down into the kitchen to give her the four pounds rent, just as she was serving up lamb casserole, and when she invited him to stay and share it with her, he accepted so quickly that she felt guilty, for perhaps, he went without an evening meal altogether. She decided to offer him the use of the kitchen, when a moment should arise which seemed suitable.

But a moment did not arise. Instead, Mr Curry came down two or three evenings a week and shared her meal, she got used to shopping for two, and when he offered her an extra pound a week, she accepted, it was so nice to have company, though she felt a little daring, a little carefree. She heard her mother telling her that the meals cost more than a pound a week. 'Well, I do not mind, they give me pleasure, it is worth it for that.'

One evening, Mr Curry asked her if she were good at figures, and when she told him that she had studied book-keeping, asked her help with the accounts for the kitchen utensil customers. After that, two or three times a month, she helped him regularly, they set up a temporary office on the dining-room table, and she remembered how good she had been at this kind of work, she began to feel useful, to enjoy herself.

He said, 'Well, it will not be for much longer, Miss Fanshaw, the summer is almost upon us, and in the summer, of course, I am self-employed.'

But when she opened her mouth to question him more closely, he changed the subject. Nor did she like to inquire whether the firm who supplied him with the cleaning utensils to sell, objected to the dearth of summer orders.

Mr Curry was an avid reader, 'in the winter', he said, when he had the time. He read not novels or biographies or war memoirs, but his encyclopedia, of which he had a handsome set, bound in cream mock-leather and paid for by monthly instalments. In the evenings, he took to bringing a volume down to the sitting-room, at her invitation, and keeping her company, she grew used to the sight of him in the opposite armchair. From time to time he would read out to her some curious or entertaining piece of information. His mind soaked up everything, but particularly of a zoological, geographical or anthropological nature, he said that he never forgot a fact, and that you never knew when something might prove of use. And Esme Fanshaw listened, her hands deftly fringing a lampshade – it was a skill she had acquired easily – and continued her education.

'One is never too old to learn, Mr Curry.'

'How splendid that we are of like mind! How nice!'

She thought, yes, it is nice, as she was washing up the dishes the next morning, and she flushed a little with pleasure and a curious kind of excitement. She wished that she had some woman friend whom she could telephone and invite round for coffee, in order to say, 'How nice it is to have a man about the house, really, I had no idea what a difference it could make.' But she had no close friends, she and her mother had always kept themselves to themselves. She would have said, 'I feel younger, and it is all thanks to Mr Curry. I see now that I was only half-alive.'

Then, it was summer. Mr Curry was out until half past nine
or ten o'clock at night, the suitcase full of brooms and brushes
and polish was put away under the stairs and he had changed
his clothing. He wore a cream linen jacket and a straw hat
with a black band, a rose or carnation in his buttonhole. He
looked very dapper, very smart, and she had no idea at all
what work he was doing. Each morning he left the house
carrying a black case, quite large and square. She thought, I
shall follow him. But she did not do so. Then, one evening in
July, she decided to explore, to discover what she could from
other people in the town, for someone must know Mr Curry,
he was a distinctive sight, now, in the fresh summer clothes.
She had, at the back of her mind, some idea that he might be
a beach photographer.

She herself put on a quite different outfit – a white piqué dress
she had bought fifteen years ago, but which still not only fitted,
but suited her, and a straw boater, edged with ribbon, not unlike
Mr Curry's own hat. When she went smartly down the front path,
she hardly dared to look about her, certain that she was observed
and spoken about by the neighbours. For it was well known now
that Miss Fanshaw had a lodger.

She almost never went on to the promenade in the summer.
She had told Mr Curry so. 'I keep to the residential streets, to
the shops near home, I do so dislike the summer crowds.' And
besides, her mother had impressed on her that the summer
visitors were 'quite common'. But tonight walking along in the
warm evening air, smelling the sea, she felt ashamed of that
opinion, she would not like anyone to think that she had been
brought up a snob – live and let live, as Mr Curry would tell
her. And the people sitting in the deckchairs and walking in
couples along the seafront looked perfectly nice, perfectly
respectable, there were a number of older women and families

with well-behaved children, this was a small, select resort, and charabancs were discouraged.

But Mr Curry was not to be seen. There were no beach photographers. She walked quite slowly along the promenade, looking all about her. There was a pool, in which children could sail boats, beside the War Memorial, and a putting green alongside the gardens of the Raincliffe Hotel. Really, she thought, I should come out more often, really it is very pleasant here in the summer, I have been missing a good deal.

When she reached the putting green she paused, not wanting to go back, for her sitting-room was rather dark, and she had no real inclination to make lampshades in the middle of July. She was going to sit down, next to an elderly couple on one of the green benches, she was going to enjoy the balm of the evening. Then, she heard music. After a moment, she recognized it. The tune had come quite often through the closed door of Mr Curry's bedroom.

And there, on a corner opposite the hotel, and the putting green, she saw Mr Curry. The black case contained a portable gramophone, the old-fashioned kind, with a horn, and this was set on the pavement. Beside it was Mr Curry, straw hat tipped a little to one side, cane beneath his arm, buttonhole in place. He was singing, in a tuneful, but rather cracked voice, and doing an elaborate little tap dance on the spot, his rather small feet moving swiftly and daintily in time with the music.

Esme Fanshaw put her hand to her face, feeling herself flush, and wishing to conceal herself from him: she turned her head away and looked out to sea, her ears full of the sentimental music. But Mr Curry was paying attention only to the small crowd which had gathered about him. One or two passers by, on the opposite side of the road, crossed over to watch, as Mr Curry danced, a fixed smile on his elderly face. At his feet was an upturned bowler hat, into which people dropped coins, and when the record ended, he bent down, turned it over neatly, and began to dance again. At the end of the second tune, he packed the gramophone up and moved on, farther down the promenade, to begin his performance all over again.

She sat on the green bench feeling a little faint and giddy, her heart pounding. She thought of her mother, and what she would have said, she thought of how foolish she had been made to look, for surely someone knew, surely half the town had seen Mr Curry? The strains of his music drifted up the promenade on the evening air. It was almost dark now, the sea was creeping back up the shingle.

She thought of going home, of turning the contents of Mr Curry's room out onto the pavement and locking the front door, she thought of calling the police, or her Uncle Cecil, of going to a neighbour. She had been humiliated, taken in, disgraced, and almost wept for the shame of it.

And then, presently, she wondered what it was she had meant by 'shame'. Mr Curry was not dishonest. He had not told her what he did in the summer months, he had not lied. Perhaps he had simply kept it from her because she might disapprove. It was his own business. And certainly there was no doubt at all that in the winter months he sold cleaning utensils from door to door. He paid his rent. He was neat and tidy and a pleasant companion. What was there to fear?

All at once, then, she felt sorry for him, and at the same time, he became a romantic figure in her eyes, for he had danced well and his singing had not been without a certain style, perhaps he had a fascinating past as a music hall performer, and who was she, Esme Fanshaw, to despise him, what talent had she? Did she earn her living by giving entertainment to others?

'I told you so, Esme. What did I tell you?'

'Told me what, mother? What is it you have to say to me? Why do you not leave me alone?'

Her mother was silent.

Quietly then, she picked up her handbag and left the green bench and the promenade and walked up through the dark residential streets, past the gardens sweet with stocks and roses, past open windows, towards Park Walk, and when she reached her own house, she put away the straw hat, though she kept on the dress of white piqué, because it was such a warm night. She went down into the kitchen and made coffee and set it, with a plate of sandwiches and a plate of biscuits, on a tray, and presently Mr Curry came in, and she called out to him, she said, 'Do come and have a little snack with me, I am quite sure you can do with it, I'm quite sure you are tired.'

And she saw from his face that he knew that she knew.

But nothing was said that evening, or until some weeks later, when Mr Curry was sitting opposite her, on a cold, windy August night, reading from the volume COW to DIN. Esme Fanshaw said, looking at him, 'My mother used to say, Mr Curry, "I always like a bit of singing and dancing, some variety. It takes you out of yourself, singing and dancing." '

Mr Curry gave a little bow.

NOTES

Morecambe and Wise, the Black and White Minstrels (p119)
 former variety shows (light entertainment) on television
BBC2 (p119)
 the television channel with more cultural or 'serious' programmes
the Daily Telegraph (p120)
 a 'quality' newspaper which supports right-wing (Conservative) politics
the Daily Mirror (p120)
 a tabloid newspaper which supports left-wing (socialist) politics
the Society (p127)
 a charity which provides institutional homes for children whose parents
 are dead
Doctor Crippen (p133)
 a murderer executed in London in 1910 for killing his wife

DISCUSSION

1 How does her mother's death change Esme's life?

2 When Mr Curry moves in as Esme's lodger, what advantages does the
   new arrangement have for him, and for Esme?

3 By the end of the story, do you think that Esme has finally shaken off
   her mother's domination for good, or will she still be fighting her in
   a private dialogue for the rest of her life? If she *is* now free, at what
   point in the story do you think the break comes, and what causes
   it? And is there a danger that Esme will eventually become like her
   mother?

LANGUAGE FOCUS

1 Mr Curry often speaks in clichés and uses well-known quotations.
   Find the following in the text, and explain their meaning:

     live and let live (p127)
     nation shall speak peace unto nation (p127)
     I have earned my passage at all times (p127)
     two strings to my bow (p128)
     sound in wind and limb (p129)

> *plying my other trade* (p130)
> *we are of like mind* (p137)

2 Look again at the passages where Esme is thinking about or having a dialogue with her mother. Can you describe all the emotions and states of mind Esme goes through (e.g. fear, guilt, shame, relief, anxiety, defiance)?

ACTIVITIES

1 What do you think might happen after the end of the story? Write another paragraph to finish the story in, for example, a year's time. Write it from Esme's point of view, including her thoughts as well as any events. Does she marry Mr Curry? Does she become a partner in his song and dance act, or just continue to make lampshades and cook his breakfasts and dinners?

2 Write Mr Curry's diary for the day he arrives at Esme's house. Describe Esme and the house in the way you think he would see them, and include his reasons for not telling her about his summer work. What do you think he deduces about Esme's mother?

IDEAS FOR COMPARISON ACTIVITIES

1 In the stories *Same Time, Same Place* and *A Bit of Singing and Dancing*, what similarities or differences are there between Esme and Miss Treadwell, and Mr Curry and Mr Thornhill?

2 Which of these two stories do you prefer, and why?